# Volunteering in Nepal
# Loitering in Lucknow

## Mark Sconce

ISBN  978-1-959457-24-4

Page 89 Himalayas photo thanks to dreokt

Published in the United States by
Blue Jay Ink

# Volunteering in Nepal
# Loitering in Lucknow

# Contents

Hill Brahmins

# Dedication

Dedicated with genuine thanks and love to my dear sister, Terry Kleid, a mountain trekker who periodically prodded me to publish and enthusiastically backed me in the project. Also, to longtime friend and mentor, Professor Jim Falen, and his wife, Eve, for seriously suggesting I write the book, encouraging me along the way, and calling to my attention sundry glitches. My sincere thanks, amigos, with deep affection.

Add to these three stalwarts, my fellow/sister workshop writers who critiqued most every vignette and kindly gave me valuable suggestions, particularly the Glossary words, which, in some cases, don't pretend to be equivalent English translations but rather my sense of them 60 years later. (How do you translate cheeze-beeze, my favorite, with daliki-daliki, a close second?)

Finally, to Bell Prasad Shrestha, Mayor of Dhulikhel, Nepal and my language guru who helped me and other Volunteers on the road to Kathmandu and beyond. Dhanyabad.

*Namaste. Let's Trek.*

# Introduction

### Peace Corps—"The toughest job you'll ever love."

Credit Ms. Winnie Kelley, a Peace Corps publicist, for that catchy yet truth-telling tag. It applied especially to me and 24 colleagues, who served two years in Nepal, considered the toughest country in Peace Corps world. We were among the first groups to live in the foothill villages of Nepal in clear view of the grandeur of the Himalayan massif with Everest on the right and Annapurna on the left. But my first year, 1967-'68, was spent living in Gaur, Nepal, a hot, dusty, flat-land town of perhaps 10,000 bordering north Bihar, India. This border area, called the Terai, is the bread basket farmland of Nepal. While not particularly happy about my posting, I eventually realized that I was lucky to be exposed to the wonder that is India, just across a border.

***

Facts about the Peace Corps that you may not know or perhaps forgotten. For instance, while President Kennedy established the Peace Corps in March of 1961, later authorized by Congress, the idea came from Minnesota Senator Hubert Humphrey who, along with United Auto Workers president, Walter Ruther, sold President Kennedy on the idea and helped push through the legislation. Critics, like Richard Nixon, predicted that it would become a "cult of escapism" and "a haven for Vietnam draft dodgers." That's why the legislation passed with the proviso that "The Peace Corps shall not be a substitute for service in the Armed Forces." But that's another story.*

President Kennedy saw the Peace Corps as a counter to the growing stereotype of the "Ugly American." It also fit nicely with his clarion call: "Ask not what your country can do for you, but what you can do for your country." I would add this: If people in emerging (developing) countries had ever seen Americans before, they saw soldiers, diplomats, businessmen, tourists, and Christian missionaries. But the early Peace Corps, largely made up of recent liberal arts graduates, idealists for the most part, offered a different American, someone who volunteered to stay in-country for two years and help out with development projects, agricultural improvements, and English lessons that I and others taught during the drawn-out monsoon months when outside projects had to be abandoned. Having just completed a legislative internship in the office of a Congressman and member of the House Foreign Affairs Committee, I knew perfectly well that the Peace Corps came about for a number of reasons, one of them being a challenge or counterpoise to Soviet incursions in places like Nepal. The Peace Corps soared on the wings of idealism but landed on the hard rock of geopolitical reality. Squeezed between India and China, Kathmandu, Nepal became a spies' nest, instead of the Asian Switzerland the Nepalese had hoped for, known for neutrality. Whenever the Indian government leaned on little brother, Kathmandu would turn north to China to enhance trade relations and development projects The Soviets were building an important east/west road at the time, and there were more than several players – a delicate balance overall. But the Peace Corps in my day was unique – not so much anymore. Like the VW, the PC has been around a long time but hasn't flourished like it did in the beginning with a can-do American spirit.

In my opinion, the name Peace Corps is confusing at best, self-defeating at worst. Any pocket-size dictionary of the sort a villager might have defines corps, as in Marine Corps, a military unit thereby creating an oxymoronic banner: Peace Platoon. It was the same sort of cultural error when, some years back, America was shipping grain to victims of natural disasters. The burlap sacks carrying corn or wheat depicted two hands shaking, something you would never see in countries like Nepal and India where palms together, heads slightly bowed is proper, respectful, and shows you care. It's clear that no cultural anthropologist attended the christening of the name Peace Corps.

Eventually, I just introduced myself as an American offering to help in development efforts. Even so, there were plenty of Nepalis and Indians who just assumed we were CIA's special undercover unit, the Peace Platoon. Other than that, I have nothing but praise for the Peace Corps, its conceptual values, its inauguration, its Nepal training program in a Davis, California migrant camp, and its support in-country as well as in Washington D.C. following my two plus years abroad.

We were so lucky to have Sargent Shriver as the first Peace Corps Director. A World War II veteran and savvy operative during Jack Kennedy's presidential campaign, he knew well the techniques of organization and got the Peace Corps on its feet in 44 countries with over 14,000 Volunteers by the time he handed the baton to Director Jack Vaughn under whom I served. Our in-country director was a lawyer from LA. named Bruce Morgan who, with his wife Betty and the kids, moved to Kathmandu. We liked and respected him and his family. He was proud to say that Peace Corps/Nepal was the only government agency to return unused monies to the United States Treasury. In one of the world's poorest countries, there isn't much to buy. We were perforce a frugal lot. Our $150 a month put us in the middle class thanks to U.S. taxpayers more used to overrides and chicanery. I salute the person who thought to include this rule: If you receive money from home during your stay, you will be sent home.

During my several years in South Asia, living, working and traveling in Nepal and India as a volunteer and later as a married visitor retracing his steps, I spoke day-to-day Nepali and picked up a smattering of Hindi because I lived on the Indian border my first year. I adapted to a Hindu culture and adopted some of the local customs. I ate my daily *dal, bhat, tarakari*, and even *gundruk*. I ate (just once) the hottest curry in India – fish curry from *Madras*. I smoked the *bidi*, shared the *chillum*, and chewed the *paan*. I listened to the *bhajan* and enjoyed the *bojan*. I trekked the Himalayan foothills and took refreshment and rest in *chia pasals* along the way. I gave *paisa* to the *sadhu* and paid the *dhobi*. I wore the *lungi*, used the *lota*, and marveled at the *lingam*. I heard the children chant their alphabet: *ka--kha ga--gha--nah*. I also heard the *ghungroos* of the *Kathak* dancer and pondered the cosmic dance of *Shiva Nataraja*.

In Calcutta, I paid my respects to Mother Teresa and accompanied a Nepali actress to a concert. I was overwhelmed by the Taj Mahal twice. I honeymooned in Kashmir and "kissed pale hands by the Shalimar." I even found time to Loiter in Lucknow. The meaning and nuances of these melodious Nepali, Hindi, and Sanskrit words will be unveiled in their appropriate contexts and settings in the following pages. (Impatient readers can turn to the Glossary.) For now, I will share an important lesson that many British colonials learned and now, too, Americans: No matter how much you know about another country, there will always be certain details, certain subtleties, certain circumstances that only the native can really understand and appreciate. Nevertheless, at the end of two years, our Peace Corps director pointed out that we were among the most sophisticated Westerners when it came to daily life in rural Nepal and northern India. That distinction used to apply to British administrators, soldiers, and merchants, many of whom spoke several of the 14 languages that now appear on the modern rupee note. But these same polyglots missed or ignored the seething under-tow that would eventually send them packing As Indian author Shashi Tharoor puts it: "all the squalid history of Indo-British personal relations -- the prosaic reality of the British baton and the white man's sneer."

The following pages offer insights into a people and a culture I respect and love. Whenever I notice a Nepali or Indian in America, I always introduce myself, have a chat, and treat them as nicely as they treated me sixty years ago. It's not uncommon to hear return volunteers say that "the people taught me more than I taught them," True. Furthermore, the experience taught me more about myself and adjusted my mindset for the better and for life.

It will not go unnoticed that I have written little about my overseer work, partly because there's not much to tell. The project overseer in the district office was a degreed mechanical engineer from India who spent his time meticulously drawing plans (blueprints) that he and I knew would never see construction anytime soon because bureaucrats in

Kathmandu were holding things up for political reasons. So, I decided to stop wasting time in the office and pedal to the people in neighboring villages on my old-fashioned Schwinn bicycle whose balloon tires fit snugly in the ox cart ruts leading to the next village. There, I could always find a bicycle repair shop and tend to bruises sustained when my dear old bike jumped the rut. (Funny thing is, when the bike is damaged beyond repair, the next best conveyance is the back of the ox-cart whose wheels caused me and Mr.Schwinn to capsize.)

In each village I visited, I had to find someone who spoke Nepali; no one spoke English. Local dialects prevailed rendering me near speechless. I eventually solved the problem by moving to a hill village the following year where Nepali, the national language, was the lingua franca. There, I was able to survey a *jethi kulo*, an irrigation system, to convey a rivulet of river water down a gradual slope to a rice paddy. But I hope my main contribution was a booklet my friend Richard and I published for Nepal overseers that contained project hardware (literally nuts and bolts) and prices from a steel manufacturer in Calcutta that agreed to work with us; FOB Nepal/India border railheads.

I will now heed Voltaire's warning: "Woe to the author determined to teach! The best way to be boring is to leave nothing out."

Boring does not describe the following vignettes.

**Namaste!**


*I come from a family of volunteers. I wanted to volunteer long before Vietnam became an issue.

# First Days

## Sojourn, Peace Corps/Nepal

When the letter arrived, post-marked Washington, D. C., I knew it had to be from the Peace Corps telling me if I had been accepted into the Thailand program. But they threw me a curve. Peace Corps said my background better suited me for Nepal, 1967. As I raced to the library to find out more about Nepal, I flashed back to that black and white Movietone footage from 1953 of Sir Edmund Hillary and Sherpa Tenzing Norgay holding on to each other at the summit, wind whipping their parka fur and their respective flags, New Zealand and Nepal atop Mt. Everest.

The library didn't have much, but I was able to discover that Nepal is about the size of Georgia and lies between India and Tibet. It's a rice economy and much of Nepal is semi-tropical, which means mangos, bamboo, orchids, lychee nuts, and vegetables you've never seen before. It remains the only officially Hindu country in the world and that includes India. During my time, Nepal was a monarchy; today it has a President as head of state and a Prime Minister who governs with the advice of the Council of Ministers. It is home to the highest mountain range in the world -- the great Himalayas featuring famous peaks like Annapurna, Dhaulagiri, and Sagarmatha, which is what the Nepalese call Mt. Everest. Looking at a globe that day, I realized that if a hole were dug from my hometown, Omaha, all the way through the earth, it would arrive in rural Nepal nearly 12, 500 miles away as the crow flies. I also noted that the rupee contains one hundred paisa and that there were ten rupees to the dollar, and I would be paid 500 rupees per month for the next two years. My first job after college, you might say...

I told Peace Corps Washington YES before finding out that Nepal was considered "the toughest country in Peace Corps world" in terms of poverty, filth, disease, climate, monsoon rigors, and rugged terrain. Not that those things would have made a difference. I was excited to go. I didn't even wait for the commencement ceremonies featuring Coretta Scott King at Antioch College before saying goodbye to family and friends and traveling to Davis, California for three months' training. My friends, by the way, thought I was serving two years in Naples.

Training camp turned out to be a migrant workers' camp just outside Davis, California. Barrack bunk beds for eight volunteers plus one cot for the native Nepali, Bell Prasad Shresta, who taught us his language and tried his best to answer our many questions in his broken English. Technical training included surveying, irrigation canals, tube wells, and pumps. They also taught us how to wring a chicken's neck, a useful skill in rural Nepal. Nepali derives from Sanskrit and, although it shares a number of words with Hindi, a Hindi speaker can't really understand Nepali. Therefore, I was not entirely happy when told that my post for two years would be Gaur on the Indian border where most folks speak something other than Nepali—Hindi, Maithili, Bhojpuri, and my favorite, Tharu, because the Tharu chief once paid me a visit.

We 25 Volunteers finally boarded a flight to Calcutta via Tokyo, Hong Kong, Rangoon and Bangkok. We left San Francisco in balmy weather. That would soon change. After many restless, cramped, introspective hours, we landed at Dum Dum Airport, Calcutta, named after the dum dum bullets stored in a depot there during the "Good War." The long bus ride to the Great Eastern Hotel at four in the morning was instructive if you've never been to India. As dawn crept forward, we could better see the buildings and the sidewalks where people lay sleeping clothed in ragged saris and wrap-around dhotis, not pajamas and lingerie. The suffocating heat would soon enough become oppressive as the morning advanced. The approaching huge city looked like a war zone, which expanded with the first rays of a September morn. I had to rub my eyes not just because of exhaustion. Piles of menacing debris and rubble lay about and many buildings looked as though they were burned out, crumbling or sagging. An alarming shabbiness and hopelessness pervaded the route. But look, there's a sacred cow contentedly chewing gutter garbage, un-tethered and untouched even by untouchables.

When we reached the Great Eastern Hotel, we were greeted by elegant, handsome, mustachioed footmen wearing elaborate, colorful and plumed turbans. Jaunty red and gold tasseled cords ran through their epaulets, and their crisp white uniforms reeked of the Raj. Yes, we were tired after the long flight, but my Cincinnati friend, Dick Nations, had another thought besides sleep. "Sconce, this is a rare opportunity to watch Calcutta wake up. We'll never have another chance, and we can sleep anytime."

Let's go, I said! And so, the two intrepid Midwesterners set out on foot as Aurora's pink fingers penetrated into the side streets of the multi-million megapolis. Folks were still sleeping or just waking up on Calcutta's sidewalks. Children still nestled in their mothers' bosoms. Other mothers were firing up the little street braziers used to cook rice. And we even witnessed, albeit obliquely, a baby being born. We also saw what had to be a recent death—an old man who probably died during the night on his hard sidewalk bed. Gargle water was being spat into the street and bodily functions were happening before our eyes. We suddenly came upon a street that contained, literally, a mountain of odorous garbage with women and children climbers carefully picking a bit here and a tidbit there. Rats? Of course.

Our appearance in this Calcutta neighborhood attracted immediate attention. We were soon besieged by street urchins, hands out, crying *O, sahib, baksheesh, baksheesh.* We couldn't help noticing that several of these young beggars, boys and girls, were missing a hand or an eye, and we favored them in our giving. We later learned that their handlers had purposely maimed these orphans to make them appear more pitiful. We also learned that you can't keep handing out paisa all morning and expect to have taxi fare home.

Yes, we were lost and really tired. But we finally found our beds in the Great Eastern Hotel through the help of a rickshaw-wallah who took up the staffs and, barefoot, pulled us to the Great Eastern.

* * *

Late the next morning, our plane lifted north to Kathmandu flying right at the Great Himalayan massif. What a sight for a young man from Nebraska---The Great Plains! All 25 of us were glued to the portals. The airport up ahead covered an oval mesa overlooking the Kathmandu Valley. The runway suddenly didn't look long enough for our carrier. The enormous Himalayan foothills loomed. We carefully touched down. Two parachutes immediately deployed to slow us to a manageable taxi before going over the edge. "Welcome to Tribhuvan International Airport, Kathmandu, Nepal. King Mahendra welcomes you to his kingdom (a kingdom that holds sacred the divine right of kings).

We soon found ourselves in yet another fine hotel famous for the Yak and Yeti Bar and where we were housed for a few days before trekking or traveling to our respective posts. During that week we met with Peace Corps officials, American Embassy officials, and His Majesty's government officials. I still remember the Peace Corps doctor's exhortation: "Cook it, peel it, or forget it. But don't forget your weekly malaria pill." Our training table back in Davis prepared us for the *dhal, bhat, tarkari* most Nepalis eat twice a day—lentils, rice and spiced vegetables—add chicken if you can wring its neck.

Kathmandu itself was incredibly exotic in the years before the great earthquakes. The temples, both Buddhist and Hindu, were especially magnificent, featuring the pagoda style roofs that we always thought originated in China. They didn't. Also featured on the Hindu temples were carved couples copulating in all manner of positions with divine expressions on their ancient faces. It was said that the builders lived in a time of alarming population decline, and the ruler therefore ordered such erotic temple carvings to encourage his subjects to "be fertile and increase," as the old Bible once enjoined. (Genesis 1:28)

The other theory is anti-erotic, you might say. To protect against lightning strikes, temple priests ordered lascivious scenes to be carved on the temple's face. Seems the goddess of lightning is a prude and would be repelled by such carvings. But God knows what the clergy had in mind 500 years ago. Kathmandu itself, according to the latest archeological record, is over 2000 years old.

I especially liked the evenings when you could hear the religious chants and music and smell the incense wafting through the bazaar. Hindu and Buddhist priests even invited me to sit with them and appreciate the musicians. The beautiful bhajan songs, the beat of the tablas, the drone of the ancient stringed sarod. Buddhist prayer flags and prayer wheels touched me...

Finally came the day when the Peace Corps driver told me to join him for a jeep ride south to a Peace Corps field office in Birgunj just across the border from an Indian railhead. There is no railroad in Nepal, not even a spur. So to get to my post, I would have to cross into India, board a train headed east and, four hours later, disembark in the small Indian town of Bairgania. From there I would make my way in a tanga, a horse drawn cart, for the hour long ride to Gaur, Nepal, my post for the first unbelievable year.

Next day, I presented my passport to the border officer and crossed into India where I boarded the train and struggled with my two Army duffle bags, a backpack and sleeping bag. The railcar I chose was filled with Indian gentlemen sitting on two long benches with an aisle in between. I sat in the only seat left and looked across the aisle at the men seated opposite. They tried their best to be cool, barely acknowledging my presence as the only Westerner on the train. I knew they were wondering why anyone like me would be traveling in this Indian backwater, Bihar, India's poorest and most conservative state, a state where a Brahmin wouldn't even think about drinking water from a well on which an untouchable had cast his shadow.

At one of our stops, a frightened lady climbed barefoot aboard clutching a baby to her soiled sari. She cowered on the floor in a corner. A distressed mother, I thought, so I got up and motioned her to my seat. She shrank back into the corner with a horrified look and pressed her child closer. Suddenly, with a perfect British accent, a gentleman reading the Hindu Times said, "She does not deserve a seat, Sir. She does not have a ticket. Come and sit by me." I thanked him and sat down, part embarrassed, part bemused. We chatted all the way to Bairgania where I detrained, located a worthy tanga wallah (horse taxi) and set off for my post, Gaur, in the Kingdom of Nepal. As the horse entered dusty Main Street, I began to notice splotches of red in the dust. Lots of them and, just ahead, I saw the reason why. A merchant emerged from his shop, stood on the curb, and spat a gob of red into the street. Tuberculosis, I thought. I'm entering a TB zone. My emaciated horse, head down, clopped on to the magic kingdom. A Bollywood song blared from a loudspeaker into the gathering dusk. I can still hear the tune, the words I learned later. **Gareebo** *ke su no, O tumhari sunega*…If you give a single paisa to a poor man, you'll receive 10,000 from heaven…

Kathmandu street scene

# Rautahat Rasslin'

I have described the journey from Kathmandu to my post on the border of India and Nepal: A memorable train trip followed by an even more memorable tonga trip to my new post, i.e. a horse-drawn cart to Gaur, Nepal, my Peace Corps posting for two-years. There, I was supposed to help out the overseer for district development projects such as road improvements, tube wells, pumps and even bridges. The latter were more important in Nepal's rugged foothills than in the flatlands bordering India, the breadbasket of Nepal. I had the pleasure of working with an Indian engineer and wonderful gentleman from Kerala in the extreme south of India. He was lucky to find an engineer's job in southern Nepal! Turned out, he had things under control and didn't really need me.

But first, I had to lease and settle into two rooms in a concrete rice mill and atrium complete with a courtyard surrounded by rooms belonging to the owner's family and their servants. One of my rooms was empty, the other room outfitted with a huge wooden chifferobe that had seen better days and a large wooden table, knee-high. That, along with a brass chamber pot *(lota)*, added a new dimension to my life what with no running water until you vigorously pumped the handle of the tube well in the courtyard. A young lad, Pradeep Kumar, offered to help me find a bed and a desk. (Youngsters, I've discovered, are more patient than their elders with a newcomer whose language ability is rudimentary.) We secured a bed, a cot really, with webbing stretched between its frames. Mattresses didn't exist; box springs, a mystery. The used wooden desk was high enough to accommodate my knees and large enough to accommodate my kerosene lamp and a few books. (*The Dubliners* and *Speak Nepalese* by Bell Prasad Shrestha whom I came to know and very much admire to this day).

Sixty years have passed, so I forget exactly how it happened that a wrestling match was proposed between me (Makur Bahadur by this time) and the champion wrestler of Rautahat District where I was stationed. A fellow Volunteer happened to be in town and thought the wrestling match was a great idea as it would draw a crowd and introduce me to town folks and villagers alike. They would view me as a good sport and a friend of the people. So I agreed, even though I was more a boxer than a wrestler. A date, time, and place were proposed and posted. I had no idea what to expect, but judging from the physiques and musculature of the men around me, I felt fairly confident of my strength and athletic prowess. I did however wrestle with the idea of winning the match and how that would be perceived by the spectators. Even Senator Fulbright's recently published book came to mind: *The Arrogance of Power*. I decided to "take a fall."

The day arrived. Citizens of Gaur and villagers from around Gaur gathered on a greensward all chattering and raising expectations. It was hot because it's always hot on the Indian border. I was the first combatant to arrive and take the field, bare-chested, loins girded, boxing trunks deployed, and an amiable countenance. As I raised my arms in recognition of a few scattered cheers, the Rautahat wrestling champion stepped out from the crowd. It was as though a tank had rolled into view and barely noticed the jeep opposite before turning to the adoring crowd. The cheers and applause were tumultuous and even festive. It's not often that the sons and daughters of ancient Aryans gather to watch a wrasslin' match between an American Unitarian and a Nepali Hindu cum warlord or, at least, he looked like one. My pledge to "take a fall" evaporated, and I suddenly realized that I was in for the fight of my life. I heard Grandpa Alva's sensible counsel: *Just do your best, son.* So I did and got immediately put down to earth amid loud applause. My opponent glistened in sweat and glowed with pride. I jumped to my feet and faced him for a second round. *When you're playing a losing game, change your strategy.* I did just that and began to circle him, crouched and ready to spring. Because he was so muscle-bound and short on flexibility, he didn't move as fast as I, Makur Bahadur (which means Brave Jupiter). And brave I was, even as I let him win the second round. Afterwards we became buddies. I still remember his name: Ram Bahadur Shrestha of the warrior caste, just like me.

# The Earring

You see some strange things during your first three months as a Peace Corps Volunteer. And if you've been assigned to a scruffy village on the Nepalese side of the border with India, you notice some strange things indeed. I was therefore fortunate to have rented my rooms from a Brahmin, Babuji, who became my surrogate father, mentor, and explainer.

One hot afternoon, sitting on the porch together watching villagers pass by on the dusty road, I asked him about the gold earrings that some Nepali men and boys wore that penetrated the fleshy cartilage at the top of the ear opposite the lobe. He explained that because infant mortality was so high in Nepal, a male child who reached adolescence was awarded a gold ring, but only if he is the sole male, the surviving male. When he learned that I was the sole, surviving male in my family, he insisted I wear the gold earring, and he knew just the right person to pierce my ear. Two years loomed ahead of me, so I thought, well, when in Naples…

Several days later, arrangements were made, and I found myself in a thatched roof hut sitting on a high stool waiting patiently for the procedure. The cooling monsoon rains were just around the corner but yesterday, today and the next day were as hot as a crematorium. Suddenly, a figure in a sari appeared, and I had to do a double take. If you ever tried to imagine what a crone looks like, this lady fit the bill. She wasn't a day under ninety but possessed a winning and reassuring smile. She also possessed a large needle in her gnarly fingers about the length of a toothpick, and, like a toothpick, thickened some in the middle. I shuddered a little and shuddered even more when she pulled a thread from the decorative yarn adorning her pigtail and began threading the needle. There was no attempt to sterilize the needle or thread. The Nepalese language doesn't even have a word for germ…

A brief minute later, she was piercing the top of my right ear, which I didn't much feel, but as the needle pushed through and into the thick middle, I came right up off the stool like a stuck pig. My crone finished her penetration with a smile and the words **deri ramro** -- very good. She left a little circle of thread to make sure the hole remained open until I could replace it with the gold ring. I smeared the area with ointment of some kind, to no avail.

Babuji said he knew a reputable jeweler just across the Nepal/India border. The next afternoon, I entered the shop of Ram Bahadur who was sitting near a fire pit with one foot operating a bellows to keep the fire white hot. After we agreed on a price, he proceeded to super heat a small cube of gold in a mould until it was molten. As the gold cooled, he teased out a ring in the shape of a teardrop and let it cool before inserting it in my ear hole. He twisted the ends to make it permanent.

Even though the resulting infection was red, swollen, and painful, I later realized that choosing to wear a Nepali earring was among my better decisions. For the next two years, it opened doors, prompted questions and conversations and caused a stir wherever I travelled in Nepal. It gave strangers permission to ask me about the ring in an American ear and, by the way, how's your family?

Back in Washington D.C., Peace Corps offices, I was advised to remove the ring before flying home to Omaha. "There's a good jeweler just down the block, Mr. Sconce."

# Where's the Beef?

Several decades ago, well-meaning, good-hearted Nebraska legislators passed a bill, signed into law that, from that day forward, our license plates would herald the one thing we could truly brag about: Beef. Like Georgia peaches, Idaho potatoes, or Maine lobsters, Nebraska beef was our pride, partly due to our nickname, The Cornhuskers. Indeed, it was that very corn fed to cattle their whole lives that produced a steak with a heavenly flavor, a steak you could cut with your fork. Sure enough The Beef State began to appear on thousands of vehicles in Omaha where I lived. But it didn't take long before some sensitive citizens complained and rightly so when they pointed to ambulances or hearses on their way to cemeteries both bearing the boast: **The Beef State.**

The law was not renewed. Today we are simply Cornhuskers representing the state wherein certain recognizable figures were born or raised: President Gerald Ford, Darryl Zanuck, the Hollywood producer who introduced us to Shirley Temple and Betty Grable, Hollywood stars Henry Fonda and Marlon Brando, human rights activist, Malcolm X and, of course, Johnny Carson. They all moved away to attain their fame, except steak-lover, Warren Buffet, the Oracle of Omaha. Nebraska: "A place to come from and a place to die," wrote Theodore Sorrenson, President Kennedy's speech writer from Lincoln, Nebraska and Letitia Baldridge, Jackie Kennedy's personal assistant from Omaha.

But I digress. We were talking about beef. One little memory captures its prevalence, popularity and pervasive influence. Our Grandfather used to take the family to an Omaha restaurant, oddly named The Sparetime Café and known for its steaks. We noticed that certain of the clientele were being led away to a room in the back of the kitchen. We children wanted to know why. What we saw through the big window was a fully-dressed-out carcass hanging from a meat hook in a temperature controlled room. The customer was pointing to an area on Bossy's flank (I think it was a Porterhouse), and Voila! That is what appeared on his dinner plate shortly after. Today, it's Omaha Steaks International.

Peace Corps/Washington, D.C. Was it an accident, a clerical error, a lost document or just plain cruelty that sent a poor Cornhusker to serve two years in the only part of the world where the cow is sacred, like Mother. As one sari-clad, barefoot lady with a water jug on her head exclaimed, "Is it true that in America you eat your Mother!?"

My physical need for beef became apparent just months after settling into my two rooms in Gaur, Nepal on the border of India where the humped-back Brahman bull originated. (Looks good enough to eat!) Also apparent was the physical difference between Hindus and Muslims. They dressed differently, they washed their hands differently, and, most of all, Muslims ate beef. An ill-considered plan began to take shape. Ill-considered because an unwritten law said "Don't lay a hand on our sacred cattle."

I made it a point to introduce myself to a Muslim in India. I set my sights on a likely collaborator—young, modern-minded, working class. Abdullah was his name. He came from a family whose lineage stretched back to the Mughal rule of Shah Jahan who built the Taj Mahal. I told him of my need. He laughed and said, *Salaam*. I'll do it.

We picked a moonless night where only a tiny torch would light the way. No electricity in Gaur ensured a stygian night at 3:00 a.m. when Nepalese were sound asleep. I hustled quietly to the border about a mile from our village. I waited and waited, all the while fearing an arrest by the morality police, Bovine Division. Abdullah finally arrived. *As-Salaam-Alaikum.* Good evening. I handed him the agreed 300 rupees, and he handed me a filthy rag full of bloody fresh beef. So desperate was my need that I actually thanked him.

Darkest before dawn, I returned safely to my digs, rewrapped what I reckoned was a Porterhouse and hid the beef out of reach of the flies and the pye-dogs. That weekend, a few fellow Volunteers came to town to relax in their rented house with an outside fire pit. While scolding me for my derring-do, they hailed the prize and looked forward to the unexpected tenderloin. We waited until dark before lighting the fire pit, and we cooked that bloody beef to a fare-thee-well. Anticipation was high. The first bite was a trip back home. But then the palate spoke. Not only were the taste and texture alarming, but we noticed that the more we chewed the larger it got. We ended our meal early, sorely disappointed.

Thus began my love affair with goat meat and its internal organs, especially when curried. Namaste!

# The Elephant in the Wedding

Toward the end of my first year in Peace Corps/Nepal, as my language skills improved, I became aware of domestic turmoil taking place within the family compound where we all lived. Babu, my surrogate father, was a Brahmin and the owner of the rice mill in the town of Gaur, Nepal, a half-hour walk from the Indian border. Babu's problem had to do with the impending wedding of his third daughter, Prithi, 16 years-old. His two elder daughters were already married. Babu finally took me aside and explained his dilemma. Because of Nepal's custom of delivering a dowry to the husband's family, and because those same kin were due to arrive the next day to negotiate the dowry, Babu was nervous because he knew that they held the whip hand. The wedding banns had already been posted, and young Prithi and her friends were more than a little excited. Babu asked if I would care to attend the meeting. "You'll see just how greedy and grasping the groom's family really is." Perhaps he thought that my mere presence as the only six-foot American in town would intimidate the opposition and enhance his own persona. He would be wrong.

The negotiating party arrived on time. The groom's father and uncle were Brahmins, of course, because same-caste, arranged marriages are the rule in South Asia and have been for thousands of years. The glint in the brothers' eyes foreshadowed a relentless avarice, and the next three hours were excruciating as Babu watched his nest egg slip away. The groom's proxies insisted on bicycles for every man in the family and expensive new saris for the women. The ladies also needed new and colorful glass bangles. The priest, the feast, and the entertainment were a given. And don't forget the servants. But the most contentious wrangle was saved for the number of rupees in cold cash. Ouch! The meeting ended on a sour note…

The wedding day arrived. The week before was filled with preparations of dress, decorations, and food. Banana leaves would serve as plates for the fifty-some guests, many of them rice farmers with their families from surrounding villages, Babu's customers. When we finally settled (cross-legged on a canvas underlay), the formalities began with chants and prayers, particularly to Parvati, the benevolent goddess of fertility, beauty, marriage and more. The god of erotic love and pleasure was invoked, namely, Kama from which we get the Kama Sutra. (The Splitting Bamboo position is not recommended for folks over 60.) The groom, a handsome young fellow dressed in a white dhoti and beige tunic, arrived and stood his ground. Like foghorns, the conch shells sounded to announce the entry of the bride, Prithi, dressed in a brilliant red sari with exquisite bridal makeup, gold forehead ornament, nose ring, and filigree necklace. Her mother, sisters and girlfriends ushered her onto center stage. One of the priests tended there a fire pit where he ritualistically scattered rice and a powder that caused multi-colored flames to flare (chilli-milli), all the while intoning ancient incantations that only a Sanskrit scholar could translate.

The senior Brahmin priest conducted the wedding. By tradition, the bride is veiled until the pledges are completed. The new husband lifts her veil and beholds her for the first time. (At least that's the way it supposed to be, but the kids ignored the rule. Prithi could be seen peeking through a crack in the door as He walked down the dusty street, and Prithi's black and white photo somehow made it into the husband's hands.) One of the priests stooped to tie her hem to the border of his dhoti, which is where we get the expression: "They tied the knot." The young couple were finally married; it was time for feasting. Steaming rice, black lentils, roti bread, mango pickles, curried pumpkin and tomatoes. None of the wedding party expected or received meat of any kind.

Our attention was drawn to a makeshift stage where dancers were warming up. Three men dressed and elaborately made up as women put on a wildly entertaining show to the delight of both adults and children. I later found out that such dancers are recognized as a distinct caste that's been around for centuries. They put on shows for weddings, festivities, and auspicious events of any kind. At the end of their show, another show arrived: A mahout, dressed to the nines, guided his fully-grown, caparisoned elephant into our welcoming crowd. He trumpeted his happiness to be invited. The children were delighted to learn that his name was Raja, king of the beasts. Thus ended the day on a happy note.

In some ways, I too felt like the elephant in the wedding…

### Epilogue

Some months after the wedding, Amma, my surrogate mother, came to me weeping. I tried to calm her with a cup of chai. When she had collected herself, she explained that the law in Nepal states that if a wife can't give a male child to the family, Babu can legally wed another wife who might give him a son. The new wife was expected to arrive the next day and occupy the marital bed---not a bed of roses!

# Tarzan Comes to Delhi

Not many months into my two-year commitment to Peace Corps/Nepal, I realized that the short walk to the border held many treasures on the other side in the dusty little town of Bairgania, India. A shabby little town but less shabby than my own town just across the border, Gaur, Nepal. Bairgania's main lure was electricity, something, except for the rice mill, we didn't have in Nepal.

The customs checkpoint back then (60 years ago) was a soldier in Khaki uniform sitting on a chair beneath a broad black umbrella to ward off the sun's fierce rays. He checked my passport once, and I never had to show it again, just a wave and a smile. "Namaste, Ramji."

It was in Bairgania that I drank my first cold beer in three months.

I found the lonely bottle in a pharmacy refrigerated along with various medicines. It was also in Bairgania that I saw my first Indian movie,

*Tarzan Comes To Delhi* starring Dara Singh, a dead ringer for Tarzan of the Apes.

I arrived at show time, the only Westerner in a little crowd of perhaps a hundred movie-goers. The main floor was reserved for men, some quite boisterous. The women were relegated to a little half mezzanine over by one wall, the Sari seats. Seems Mr. Singh was both a hero and a heartthrob; the

cinema was full, which added to the sweltering heat lessened only slightly by half-dozen electric ceiling fans, blades revolving grudgingly. A bottle of water and a bag of roasted chickpeas and lentils accompanied me to my seat. The lights finally dimmed; folks quieted; the movie began.

Midway, after a scene full of Bollywood dancing and singing, Jane, played by gorgeous Mumtaz Askari, finds herself alone with Tarzan. Not always, but in those days, the government put a lid on kissing in public and kissing on-screen. The audience was well aware of this prohibition but expectant nonetheless as an intimate moment arrived, and eye lashes began to flutter. Then, just as their lips closed to within an inch, the electricity failed.

A riot ensued!

The men were mad as hell; the women clucked furiously. Windows were opened to let in light and perhaps a passing breeze to mitigate the fetid heat. A group of young men in the center section began to yell Hindi obscenities while ripping out the seats, backs included. As the fan blades came to rest, one rioter, with the help of his mates, stood on the back of his chair, reached up and bent down the metal fan blades. As he did so, the electricity suddenly came back on, and the bent blades nearly tonsured him.

Order was quickly restored. Windows closed; seats replaced; quiet returned. Tarzan and Jane resumed their "relationship" sans smooch. I watched this cinematic moment truly mesmerized. While munching spicy lentils, I suddenly realized that *Tarzan Comes To Delhi* was the most exciting movie I had ever seen.

\* \* \*

# Judaism Meets Hinduism

An ecumenical moment presented itself one Sunday afternoon in a Camarillo, California park. I asked my Jewish friend, Frank Seiden, to join me in the Hindu festival of colors called Holi that takes place across South Asia each year on a different date, just like Hanukkah. As a Peace Corps volunteer in a Nepalese village on the Indian border, I experienced my first Holi festival when the villagers woke me one March morning and, while in my jammies, insisted I drink a glass of water buffalo milk. No one thought to tell me it was laced with ganja….They threw bright powdered colors all over me then playfully dragged me off my porch and hustled me into the town square where other villagers waited. Folks were definitely in a festive mood, much like that of Mardi Gras. But instead of throwing Mardi Gras beads, they were throwing bright red, pink, and yellow colors at each other---colors in powder and liquids squirting multi-colors---Joyful! Joyful! Joyful! Then they persuaded me to demonstrate the Twist (like we did last summer). I did so, surrounded by gleeful villagers and invigorated by Chubby Checker blaring over a loudspeaker. They liked my dance routine and insisted I have a glass of roxi, the native brew. I didn't really need it, but when in Rome…I staggered home. Just a few years earlier, First Lady Jackie Kennedy visited India at Holi time. She joined in but only in a limited way so as not to stain her Oleg Cassini dress.

The dress code in the Camarillo park was less formal. Although a few saris and Punjabi outfits appeared, most folks dressed to meet the chill of the day. Dozens of Indians and Indian families swelled to dozens more as the afternoon wore on. Just like India, folks were playing Holi in a joyful, festive mood. Dancing and singing (just like the Jewish horah) enhanced the afternoon along with Indian cuisine---the saffron biryani, the vegetable samosa, the mango lassi, all served by the Fresh Curry Chefs restaurant. My Jewish friend, indeed, the only Jew there, was soon multi-colored from head to shoes. He, in turn, girded his 94-year-old loins and began throwing yellow powder at Hindu immigrants from 12,500 miles away; from the wonder that is India. Holi is a time to make friends and a time to make amends. It's a leveler among the various castes in India and Nepal. A lower caste person can throw color at a Brahman and not be punished. In turn, we found out that a Jew can throw color at a Hindu and not be chastened. Imagine then the color of joy, the color of happiness, the color of friendship and love, there to paint your life. Namaste/Shalom.

# A Knock on the Door

In Peace Corps world, it is widely acknowledged that the "war stories" that came out of Nepal were the most amazing, spellbinding, and almost unbelievable unless you'd been living in a town on the Indian border one year and in a remote hill village the next. But even then... And not just the little things like gentlemen spitting red phlegm from their porches onto the dusty road below or watching two soldiers holding hands as they marched in platoon formation down that same spittle-red road. The little things like the village shaman blowing dust into the mouth of a visitor suffering from food poisoning and exactly how a doctor saved his life. (Think of a straw in a soda can.) And what about another snake-oil shaman declaring that he could heal the sick by application of the powder derived from "the horn of a fox." Nepal's daily dangers remind me of that early evening when my next sandal-clad footstep would have landed on the back of a banded-krait, a snake more poisonous than the cobra. Finally, a celestial display at the end of the day watching the sun set on one side of Mount Annapurna and the moon rise on the other side—witnessed with a family of Tibetans in a refugee camp. Buddha was there, I swear.

But there are two tales especially that deserve elaboration, one from my own experience and the second from a fellow Volunteer.

* * *

Scene: My two-room rental featuring no electricity, no running water, a rundown, heavy wooden wardrobe, and a low-slung table the size of a paw-paw patch. My newly purchased bed was more like a new-age hammock with strings for springs and no mattress -- a foreign concept. Sleep one night was interrupted by a disturbance at the foot of my sleeping bag. My flashlight beam startled two rather large, plump rats that, in turn, startled me. Next morning, I told my young helper, Pradeep Kumar, to solve the problem ASAP. It wasn't long after that we sprinkled rat poison around the baseboards. By week's end, we had results almost as good as that of the Pied Piper of Hamelin. We had eliminated the problem, but another one soon presented itself with a knock on the door. Our visitor was a tall gentleman with the bearing of a leader. In fact, he was the chief of the Tharu tribe whose communities are reckoned to be the first indigenous tribe in Nepal dating back hundreds of years. They are noted for their unusual height which finds its best expression in their tall, graceful women, especially when you see them walking in line, erect postures with tall vases of water balanced on their heads, backlit by a setting sun. Ethereal! Our caller was a Tharu chief who stated his business directly.

"It has come to my attention that you have rats. I would like to buy them. My people eat the meat."

"I'm sorry to say, sir, that they have been poisoned. We had no idea of your special food."

He acknowledged that he couldn't buy poisoned rats but asked that we not poison them in the future. We agreed and he walked off. Namaste!

* * *

The second tale involved my friend's love of Bihari mangos. Aficionados declare them the best in the world what with their golden skin, sun-kissed to perfection. The Queen of Fruits. My friend was so taken that he offered to buy a mango tree. The owner accepted his 500 Rupee offer, and my fellow Volunteer became the proud owner of a mature mango tree. The next morning, there was a knock on the door that opened on a bright-eyed, barefoot lad of twelve.

Namaste, Sahib. My name Krishna Bahadur. Can come in?"

"Sure, kid. How can I help?"

"You buy mango tree. I come with mango tree to protect from boys like me who steal mangos every year. Where will I sleep, Sahib?"

# God's Little Finger

It began in Calcutta the day after I arrived as a newly minted Peace Corps Volunteer, final destination, Kathmandu, Nepal. A luxury room awaited me in a British landmark, The Great Eastern Hotel, where a demonstration of Indian classical dancing was advertised on the mezzanine floor. At the time, I didn't know that I was witnessing Bharatnatyam, one of the nine styles of classic Indian dancing, I only knew that I was instantly captivated in the same way the Bolshoi ballet would galvanize me years later.

During the next year in Nepal, I had a chance to read more about India's classical dances and vowed to see one or more of them before returning home. Vacation time arrived; I boarded the train to Lucknow, one of Britain's important colonial outposts, now a bit faded. Lucknow I learned was home to a very famous dance school specializing in Kathak, one of the dances belonging to the classic canon.

I arrived at the school door, was greeted warmly (the temperature was 100 plus), ushered in and told to wait a moment for the Director, Mr. Sharma. He arrived clad in a traditional Indian dhoti – a white loin cloth of sorts. I instantly noticed the sacred thread athwart his chest identifying him as a Brahmin, one of the keepers of the cultural flame.

Over lunch (Basmati rice, black lentils, curried vegetables and pungent chutney), my host explained that the word **katha** means story and **kathak** means story-teller. Before Jesus, before Abraham, before Buddha, young highly trained dancers performed within Hindu temples analogous somewhat to the Romans' Vestal Virgins. Indians called them Devadasis, female servants of God dedicated to a temple for life. Their dances narrate stories from Hindu scriptures, the Mahabharata and Ramayana. They tell the tales through their eyes and brows and mouth; their hand gestures, and even finger positions. The purposeful poses, the rhythmic elements, and the mathematical precision of the feet reflect the influence of Islam during the Mughal era.

After another cup of tea, we crossed the road to a large auditorium wherein a dozen female dancers were practicing. Director Sharma beckoned one of his teachers, and she greeted him with Namaskar, a more respectful address than Namaste. Her name was Shakuntala, in her mid-twenties, training since she was five. He asked her if she would kindly give a special performance of Kathak for his new American friend. "Tell the story of Lord Krishna, the day he defeated arrogant Indra."

(Indra, the god of thunder and rain, who was punishing villagers with a devastating deluge. Krishna picks up a nearby mountain, places it on his little finger, and holds it like an enormous umbrella over the village thereby saving the people beneath.)

Palms together, head bowed, Shakuntala agreed and excused herself so that she could don her **ghungroos**, the belt of bells wrapped around each ankle. At last, barefoot, she began to dance, sheathed in a bright white sari, coal black hair shining with coconut oil, and her knowing eyes ringed in kohl, the ancient black eye cosmetic.

She was svelte, she was lithe, and she was mesmerizing. Her precise and pulsating footwork were in exact sync with the rhythms of the tabla drum and the magical strings of the sitar. Her charming posture, posed just so, her ankle bells a-jangle (she even made one bell jingle), her hands placed just so, and her omniscient expressions staggered my senses. When she finished with her little finger pointed up and a sly expression on her face looking intently at me, I nearly fell to my knees. **Namaskar**!

# Loitering in Lucknow

My train to Calcutta included a long layover in Lucknow, capital to both Nawabs and the British Raj. Well into my second year in Nepal and North India as a Peace Corps Volunteer, I looked forward to loitering in a major city (population four million), even in 100 degree heat. Besides being the capital of Uttar Pradesh and therefore home to governance, administration, and commerce, Lucknow flourished under Mughal rule and soon became the artistic and cultural centre of India synonymous with refinement and graciousness, aspects best illustrated in the story of two local Nawabs who miss their train because of their insistence that the other climb aboard first. Aspects that included song, dance, poetry, and music; stunning ancient Mughal mosques, minarets, palaces, mausoleums, and an ornate archway that leads into the city's beating heart where even more architectural wonders appear including the British Residency. When the British ruled India, Lucknow became an administrative capital. One administrative building has inscribed on its frieze: "Government Work Is God's Work." Sigh!

After a meal of lamb kebabs and biryani (native to Lucknow), I began to stroll down one street then another, a lost but not lonely Westerner. A rhythmic sound drew my attention. I followed it down a commercial street where moms and dads and kids walked from shop to shop peering inside, when suddenly I saw him. A *sadhu* walking toward me, down the middle of the street, totally nude, long, shaggy hair glistening with coconut oil, and the traditional horizontal lines on his forehead indicating that he was a devotee of Lord Shiva. Folks on the sidewalks ignored him, didn't even look up. They respected the sadhu's quest for oneness with God. East meets West on a Lucknow street. I noticed he was carrying his wooden board, the size of home plate, to squat on while eating. He wore an ecstatic expression, he chanted his mantra; he contemplated the Absolute. I suddenly felt disinclined to reach for my camera. He passed me by without a glance.

(Let's review *sadhu*. A *sadhu* is a religious ascetic we sometimes associate with yogis. He has renounced his worldly success, his material possessions, and family to become a beggar traveling from place to place. Mendicant monks, you might say. Indians of a more rational bent consider many of them simply beggars looking for a handout while masquerading as a monk. The blessings they bestow on donors therefore are bogus and deceitful. By contrast, blessings bestowed by genuine sadhus are highly sought after by both Hindus and Jains.)

I returned my attention to the rhythmic sound—bop, bop, bop. A few blocks farther brought me to its source: two gentlemen, cross-legged, clad in dhotis, bare-chested and pounding something on a wooden stump with a stout wooden paddle. Bop, bop, bop. I was baffled. In my best Hindi, I inquired. Their explanation was beyond my comprehension—something about gold and silver and fooding. One of them offered to demonstrate. He placed on the stump a cube of gold about the size of dice. He then began to pound it unmercifully. The cube began to flatten, then, flatten even more until it was the size of my hand and tissue thin. The other craftsman walloped a cube of silver to the same size and effect. He asked where I was staying. The Taj Mahal Lucknow. He recommended the restaurant there where I could see his handiwork, his fine filigree sheets of pure metal.

That evening, I ordered lamb vindaloo with a biryani side dish.

While waiting, I began to admire the photos and paintings of the Taj Mahal which, after all, was built by the Mughal emperor, Shah Jahan, as the eternal resting place for his favorite wife, Mumtaz Mahal. My entrée arrived. And there it was hugging the contours of the food, golden filigree. As preposterous as it sounds, the waiter assured me that it was okay to plunge my fork into the gold tissue and eat it along with the food. Okay, because the "gold is pure," not to mention decorative! Ah, the wonder that is India. Namaste.

* * *

# Sound, Rhythm, Meaning

Let's face it. Some languages sound better than others whether or not you understand the words and sentences. French comes to mind: Je t'aime. Je vous en prie, S'il vous plait. Also Italian: Ciao Bella, Molto bene, Arivaderchi not to mention operatic arias that live forever...

But of all the languages that best match sound to meaning, I choose Nepali and Hindi. Especially in the lyrics of songs. Take this Nepali ditty. Dhalaki, dhalaki na hirna nani. Roughly, don't walk away swaying your hips like that. Dhalaki, dhalaki describes the hips he longs to see again. Nepalis like repetitions and rhymes, much like cockney. Here's one: Rangi-changi means multi-colored like the aurora borealis; Chili-milli means flashing lights like fireworks. But the one I'll always remember is Cheeze-beez. Translation— tchotchkes, baubles, knickknacks, and gimcracks. And how do Nepalis say WOW? For nearly a thousand years, they've said Bhaprebhap or just plain Bhap!

It's fun to hear the schoolchildren walking home on a foothill path singing the Nepali alphabet, Ka, kha, ga, gha, na; cha, chha, ja, jha, ya; pa, pha, ba, bha, ma. As you can hear, all the letters end in ah. Same with Hindi. So we get Mahatma Gandhi, Buddha, Himalaya, Kamasutra (literally "Pleasure Manual,") Raja, Karma, Yoga and Ganga, the native name for the Ganges River. All melodious...even euphonious.

In India you have a vast wealth of sounds and rhythms over the millennia. On the rupee note today, you will find fourteen different languages. Once in Calcutta, I purchased an ayurvedic medicine with the Sanskrit name Mrita Sanja Bhani—to be taken at the point of death. I purchased two...

From Sanskrit to Hindi, ancient and modern, from the earliest Vedas to a Bollywood song and dance, expect conflicting perspectives. Sadhus meditating on Brahma, the Creator; gurus pondering Vishnu, the Preserver and his son Krishna, hero of the Bhagavad Gita and, of course, Shiva, the Destroyer, the swallower of Time and Ages. All these gods can come into focus when a devotee recites the universal mantra Om Mani Padme Hum. Om, a sacred symbol, Mani Padme, jewel of the lotus flower and Hum means something like the condition of Enlightenment symbolized by the lotus and the jewel of wisdom therein.

By contrast, take a typical Bollywood song like *Maito Deewana, Deewana*. "I am a mad passionate lover." Perhaps the Kamasutra comes to mind, perhaps not...

Or take this popular song where charity has its rewards:

*Tum ek paisa dogi, O das lakh a dega.* "If you give a beggar a single paisa, you'll receive ten-thousand from heaven."

But a voice from the past, no less than the word of Krishna, comes with this admonition:

On action alone be thy interest,

Never on its fruits.

Let not the fruits of action be thy motive,

Nor be thy attachment to inaction

* * *

# Say It in Sanskrit

It may not be the oldest language (Tamil enjoys that distinction), but it has been the bedrock language, the progenitor of most of India's languages today, including Bengali, Punjabi, and Hindi. Once you're in-country and somewhat settled, for example, in the Taj Intercontinental Hotel, you might look at the Indian currency given to you at the money exchange. You notice that the denominations are in different colors, which is always a good idea, but then, too, you might notice that there are 14 different languages on each of the notes, Hindi and English being the most prominent. One of those languages is Sanskrit, which is odd because we think of Sanskrit as an ancient language, like Latin, no longer in use, lost, as they say, in the mists of time. We'd be wrong. In the southwestern state of Karnataka, there are villages whose residents use Sanskrit for day-to-day communication. Elsewhere, in Hindu temples across the land, priests invoke Shiva or Vishnu in Sanskrit much as the Pope used to invoke God in Latin.

Let's look into this oddity a little closer. Linguists call Sanskrit the "mother member" of a family of languages called Indo-European because Sanskrit words can be found in Latin, Greek and other European languages. The word father, for example, is 'pitar' in Sanskrit, 'pater' in Greek and Latin, 'padre' in Spanish, 'pere' in French, and 'vader' in German.

What came before Sanskrit is a little like asking what came before the Big Bang? Professional linguists call it Vedic Sanskrit referring to the Vedas, a collection of sacred poems or hymns that were transmitted orally for hundreds of years before taking shape as a written text around 1500 BCE and whose best known Veda is the Rig Veda containing the oldest known reference to Yahweh.

From that fog emerged Sanskrit whose meaning can be translated as "pure, perfect, and polished." It's no wonder Brahmin priests co-opted Sanskrit to commune with any one of their Hindu gods. Hinduism and Sanskrit parallel each other as the centuries unfold along with other "cousin" languages, especially Hindi and Nepali. Even under Mughal (Islamic) rule where Persian was spoken at court, Sanskrit and Hinduism so intrigued Mughal rulers that they ordered their scribes to translate Hinduism's most sacred texts, texts such as the *Bhagavad Gita*, gospel to the Hindu.

In the fifth century, Kalidasa, a Sanskrit poet and playwright penned Shakuntala, a masterpiece considered by some among the hundred best books in the world.

King: It is plain that she is already wearied by watering the trees. See!
Her shoulders droop; her palms are reddened yet;
Quick breaths are struggling in her bosom fair;
The blossom o'er her ear hangs limply wet;
One hand restrains the loose, disheveled hair.

The first President of India Dr Rajendra Prasad said, "Our culture, literature and life are incomplete as long as our scholars, thinkers and educators are ignorant of Sanskrit." Mahatma Gandhi said, "No one can become an Indian and a scholar without knowing Sanskrit."

While serving in the Peace Corps, I found myself one day at an Ayarvedic pharmacy in Calcutta asking for something to ease my nagging headache. The scholarly-looking Brahman poked around his herbs, roots, and spices, and came back with just the thing. "Our medicines come from the Vedas. That's why they're called Ayarvedic. Here you are, sahib. *Mritasanjivani*. Its name in Sanskrit means

"To be taken at the point of death,"i.e. bring you back to life.

"I'll take two," I said.

Namaste.

For my understanding of such matters, I'm indebted to several scholars, all of them women.

*Historic India* by Lucille Schulberg

*India Before Europe* by Catherine B. Asher & Cynthia Talbot

*Hinduism: The Anthropology of a Civilization* by Madeleine Biardeau

*Culture of Encounters: Sanskrit at the Mughal Court* by Audrey Truschke

Pronounced ŌM, this Sanskrit symbol stands for Brahman, the Supreme Being.

# Abject Poverty

### A restaurant in Patna India

If I remember correctly, there is a maxim in the field of Sociology that says something like this: In a chaotic situation, where a crowd of people are yelling both in anger and anguish, a leader will inevitably arise and calm the uprising by organizing the group to attain what they all want. If it isn't a maxim, it should be. I saw it, as they say, with my own eyes and through the eyes of my good friend and fellow volunteer, Richard Nations (University of Pennsylvania) who, come to think of it, may have been the one who mentioned the maxim,

Where is it?? What place on earth?

The place where you will find the largest most delicious cashews on Mother Earth; a place that yields the most exotic fruit: the juicy lychee so velvety sweet; a place that produces the Queen of fruits: the pink/yellow mangoes; a place called Bihar, a state in northern India, in a city where Richard and I dined one hot afternoon in a popular neighborhood restaurant. Even for the curry gourmands we imagined ourselves, it was a memorable meal with an expert blend of spices crafted over millennia and what Europeans craved given their bland cuisine. (They didn't even have pepper or peppers.)

Richard feasted on goat curry; I on lamb curry, both dishes sprinkled with crumbly cashews, one of which is as big as your thumb. Oh, the steaming plate of perfectly cooked rice accompanied by spicy black lentils and curried pumpkin. The side dish of plain yoghurt meant to calm an overly-spiced palate competed with a dish of curried mango chutney washed down with a bottle of Flying Horse beer. Our dessert, meant to clear the palate, was rice pudding, cinnamon-laced. Completely satisfied, nay, sated, we paid and walked outside to the sound of shouting from an insistent crowd in an empty dirt lot adjacent the restaurant. The crowd of mostly women, barefoot and wearing filthy saris, surged toward the side of the building where a door opened and a restaurant employee appeared with a large container of food, much of it the leftovers from the plates of patrons like us.

We watched a near riot explode as the hungry throng, arms outstretched in supplication, became a jostling, pushing crowd preventing any food hand-outs at all. Suddenly, a young woman of about 30, shouted something, and there was a moment's pause. The sudden leader set about organizing the crowd into a relatively straight line, and the "fooding" began one by one. We even witnessed women picking up grains of rice fallen in the dust. It's one thing to read about abject poverty, quite another to witness it up close.

As if on cue and within seconds of each other, Richard burped and I belched. We exchanged an embarrassed glance. The bitter irony didn't go unnoticed. A clock tower chimed the hour. We hurried to the train station. All aboard. Next stop, Calcutta!

# Muzaffarpur

*"Who deserves the sterner blame/Though each will be a sinner:*
*She who becomes a whore for pay/Or he who pays to win her?"*
*—Sor Juana Inez de la Cruz, 17th century, Mexico*

The Peace Corps doctor was blunt. "Don't mess around these next two years whether here in Nepal or India or Bangkok unless you want to enter into a whole new universe of pain. If you thought lymphogranuloma venereum was exotic, I have news for you. There's a cornucopia of bugs out there that can eat you up and spit you out. Bugs we've never heard of…So be very careful out there so we don't have to send you home to Walter Reed with a tag on your toe that says:

Asymptomatic, non-specific disease. In other words, we don't know what the hell it is and only hope that you do…"

My friend and fellow Volunteer, Richard, and I digested that warning; then he trekked off to Dhulikhel and I to Gaur, Nepal.

Well into our second year, Richard and I were tapped to travel to Calcutta where several manufacturers of steel cable and suspension bridge hardware awaited our business. We represented His Majesty's government in Kathmandu.

After boarding the train and settling in, we noted on our map that a legendary city lay several hours down the track and where we had a long layover. We had both heard about Chaturbhujsthan, Muzaffarpur, one of India's oldest and largest red light districts. A site to behold we both were told. "Let's go just so we can say we saw it."

It so happened that Bihar's state elections were taking place the day we arrived. Communist banners, Congress Party posters and conservative Hindu party palettes painted the city and added to the already garish graffiti. Richard and I hadn't wandered too far from the train station when police stopped us and asked that we come to their station. After we explained our mission to the chief constable and brought forth His Royal Majesty's seal of approval, the chief nodded his head and welcomed us to his city. If he had added, "Be careful, it's a zoo out there," he wouldn't have been far from the truth...

Over chai and curried pumpkin and lychee nuts, we planned our next move when suddenly a gentleman appeared and introduced himself, as Indians are wont to do. He was a government worker but since it was Election Day he was enjoying a day off. He offered to show us around; we asked to see an election site and Chaturbhujsthan. He showed no surprise at our request, and he bade us follow him to a nearby polling place outside in the blazing sun. We stayed just long enough to observe that some voters in line had already voted some 30 minutes before. Our new pal, Mr. Chatterjee, explained that the ink that voter officials applied under the cuticle of each voter could be erased by rubbing the inked fingernail through coconut oil, the preferred hair dressing for so many Indian men and women. Rethinking voter fraud, we strolled over to Chaturbhujsthan, comprising not just a couple of streets but a whole and complex neighborhood cheek by jowl with ancient Hindu temples.

Every kind of prostitute presented herself in colorful diversity, not on the sidewalks or lanes, but through the large picture windows of each brazen brothel. Some girls were garlanded with ropes of jasmine flowers. A kind of cheerfulness and festive air pervaded the scene block after block, a "hey, look-me-over" festive air. When we noted the Hindu temples nearby, Mr. Chatterjee explained that in ancient India special girls were recruited to become Devi Dassis "the servants of God," somewhat analogous to Christian nuns or Vestal Virgins of Greece and Rome, the temple priestesses. But Devi Dassis were also temple dancers and singers, and it is because of them that India has such a rich tradition of classical music and dancing.

Richard and I gawked like two hicks from Ohio and Nebraska respectively. Oriental gentlemen were ogling, too, including battle-hardened Afghan fighters sporting dirty turbans, tough faces, black beards and chest bandoliers. We didn't stop to chat. Whiffs and wisps of spicy incense blended with perfumed bodies and dazzling colors of the saris, Punjabi outfits, tight blouses with glimpses of electric blue bras and exotic midriff chains. The thick smear of cosmetics clashed with the sparkling glass bangles and golden bling. Almost every bare feminine foot was graced by anklets of little silver bells and brass toe-rings.

Recent college graduates, Richard and I were especially interested in the college student brothel. It featured pretty college age girls pretending to read textbooks whilst perched seductively on bunk beds beckoning us with sultry, pouty looks, sensual glances and lascivious laughter. *Aaja Sajan Aaja*, they sang. *Aaja Sajan Aaja*. "Come love me, come love me." A teacher appeared, presumably offering prostitutorials. Meanwhile, a popular Bollywood song wailed in the distance, a young man singing *Maito Diwana, Diwana*. I am a mad, passionate lover.

Like most institutions, there existed a whore hierarchy. Lowest on the rung were the so-called ten rupee *walis*; highest on the ladder were stunning and expensive. All at once, we saw a young lady sitting on a porch facing the lane. She was obviously a Nepali woman in her mid-twenties wearing traditional jewelry and a subtle sari usually worn for ceremonies, rather like the *quinceañera* gowns. We said *Namaste, kasto chha*. She was naturally startled. I asked to come in while Richard, who spoke better Hindi than I, entered an Indian boudoir across the lane.

* * *

Her name was Hisila, a Newar from Kathmandu. Newars are to Kathmandu what Brahmins are to Boston. I looked around her single room. *Bare* best described it. Bare, except for the Shiva calendar on the wall, the keyhole toilet in one corner, a drain in the middle of the cement floor and of course a single bed. As she began to unwind her sari, I protested "No, no I just want to talk." She looked confused and a little frightened. We sat down on the bed and talked. Indeed, she was a Newari woman from Kathmandu whom the family disowned because she fell in love with some nice fellow not of her caste. Now she was paying the price, alone and stuck in cheap sex just to make ends meet. I wished her well and paid well above the going rate.

Back outside, Mr. Chatterjee said, "Let's go to my favorite brothel." Down a nondescript lane, to a nondescript door with no numbers or even a pair of sconces. Knock, knock. A gentleman of about fifty with a distinguished gray mustache opened the door and invited us into a large room with big soft pillows for our comfort in front of a large platform stage. A few finger snaps and soon food and drink appeared. A few more snaps and four musicians entered the room bearing *tablas* (drums), a *harmonium* (a small pump organ), a *sarod* (a stringed instrument) and a *bansuri* or flute. They began to tune up just like a symphony orchestra would. When they were satisfied with their instruments' sounds, they broke into a lively melody that triggered the appearance of the loveliest teenager we had ever seen. She was the very essence of beauty, grace, and style---a truly breathtaking example of Indian beauty, bejeweled and wearing a stylish sari. Anklet bells began to tinkle as she broke into a dance both energetic and sensual. We were all mesmerized, including the girl's mother who stood in the doorway wearing an expression of quiet pride. After some fifteen minutes of entertainment, the music suddenly stopped, the spell was broken, and she left the room. Her father approached and straight-forward asked for more money. We complied, and she reappeared and danced and sang some more. Our hour of departure arrived, and we left their home headed for the train station. On the way, we asked Mr. Chatterjee to further explain the exact nature of the girl's prostitution.

"That family is of an ancient caste whose forebears established the rules of their enterprise. A would-be customer over time must become a devotee of the girl and her talents. When he has demonstrated his devotion by regular visits, he is finally given permission to sleep with the beautiful daughter. I am a devotee," he asserted proudly.

*"So who deserves the sterner blame/Though each will be a sinner:*
*She who becomes a whore for pay/Or he who pays to win her?"*
—*Sor Juana Inés de la Cruz*

My village main street.

A corpse to a funeral pyre

The Buddha

East meets West

Prince Albert Museum, Mumbai

# How Now Gherao!

My friend and colleague, Richard, and I were well into our second year of service to Peace Corps/Nepal when we were tapped to travel to Calcutta on an information-gathering trip that would help Nepali civil engineers acquire products that Nepal couldn't manufacture but India could. Arrived at the Howrah train station, we decided to put up in a very basic lodging for laborers and itinerant salesmen. (No women allowed.) Our second floor room consisted of a cot on either wall with a drain in the middle of the concrete floor between us and a calendar picture of Lord Shiva on the wall instead of Jesus. Bathing and such were accomplished in the center courtyard below where several old-fashioned pumps stood tall, their iron handles at the ready. At the opposite end, a little balcony allowed us to view the bustling street scene below featuring hawkers of every stripe. We were the only Westerners in the neighborhood.

Next morning, looking our best in khaki pants and long-sleeve blue work shirts, we flagged a rickshaw for the short ride to an enormous brick business building with a sign that said Bharati Iron & Steel Mfg. (Bharat is the Sanskrit word for India.). A uniformed guard wearing a natty red turban opened the door and welcomed the two sahibs. We were led up an ornate marble staircase by an executive assistant to the mahogany office of the president. We were politely greeted by an amiable gentleman in his 60s wearing a fashionable suit from the 40s that would have elicited snickers in a New York office. Mr. Santosh Patel remarked that he hadn't had the pleasure of doing business with Americans. We thanked him, but noted that we were in town on behalf of the project overseers in rural Nepal who needed certain steel items, like steel cables, to build small suspension bridges, bridges that would connect Himalayan hill villages and increase trade thereby. He immediately understood and ordered an ever-present servant to fetch catalogues and price lists. Another servant appeared with steaming chai protected by a tea cozy, local lychee nuts, and British biscuits for our pleasure. Soon enough, we were examining hardware, literally nuts and bolts, their availability and prices, FOB the Nepali border where---

Suddenly, an assistant director with an alarmed expression dashed into the office and whispered something in the president's ear. The chief's countenance instantly changed and, as he stood up, he quickly explained that we must leave Now; else we'd be stuck in the building for days, maybe weeks. We said a quick Namaste and hustled down the hall keeping up with a servant who led us to the entrance. Once there, he gingerly opened the heavy door and there, to our astonishment, was a large crowd of angry workers and agitators yelling something we didn't understand. Our helper called it a gherao* and said we must leave immediately. Richard and I squeezed through the door ajar, ignored the raging crowd to the best of our ability and hurried down the steps to a side street and out of harm's way although nothing hostile was ever directed towards us. Twenty years earlier, when India achieved its independence, we would have been mistaken for Englishmen. Twenty-years later, we were American volunteers.

*Our Handbook for Nepali Overseers was published and distributed.

\* \* \*

Back on our street and next to our hotel, there stood a store doing a brisk business. The sign said *Dahi Kolkata* meaning curd, said to be a Calcutta specialty. We waited our turn in line with the workers in lungis, the merchants in dhotis, and the mothers in sarees, many with children in hand and on hip. First thing we noticed was the way customers discarded the empty shallow baked clay plates on which Calcutta's yellow dahi is served. Once a satisfied customer finished his dahi with the little wooden spoon provided, he simply threw the plate to the curb where it shattered into a hundred pieces. Naturally we inquired about this custom while paying for our own plates. The boss said in a broken British accent that their society needs to keep potters in business. Work is scarce for nearly a billion people.

After finishing our yellow dahi and smacking our lips, we hurled our plates to the curb just as the street sweeper appeared wielding a push broom of sturdy bristle. Viva India! Jai Hind.

*Gherao* is a Sanskrit word, which means to encircle. The workers may *gherao* the members of the management by blocking their exits and forcing them to stay inside. The main object of gherao is to inflict physical and mental torture to employers untill the demands of workers are met. It is the opposite of a lockout by management.

# The Bard of Bengal

### Rabindranath Tagore (1861-1941)

It was my third visit to the State of Bengal and its capital, Calcutta, this time for a brief vacation from my work in Peace Corps/Nepal. Indian friends made clear that Calcutta was India's culture capital. Literature and poetry, classical music and dance, singing and acting—it's all in Calcutta. Performances, concerts, readings, and recitals abound both public and private. Innovations and traditional forms coexist beautifully. One star stands out in this artistic galaxy: Rabindranath Tagore, India's outstanding creative artist.

"I am modern... I was born into a family which rebelled, which had faith in its loyalty to an inner ideal. If you want to reject me, you are free to do so. But I have my right as a revolutionary to carry the flag of freedom of spirit into the shrine of your idols—material power and accumulation." This, from a man who was raised mostly by servants and tutors in a wealthy family that prided itself on leading the so-called Bengal Renaissance by sponsoring the publication of literary magazines and hosting theatre performances and recitals of Bengali and Western classical music.

When he became the first non-European to win the Nobel Prize in Literature in 1913, the West took notice of this Bengali bard. Bengali bards were not new of course. Even illiterate wandering minstrels were capable of poems like these:

I plunged into the water like a fisherman, hoping to catch the fish of faith.

Devotion, which was my fishing net, got torn to pieces.

I only gathered some useless shells---jealousies and blames, churning the mud in vain...

* * *

Lord, the road to you is blocked by temples and mosques. I hear your call, my Lord,

But I cannot advance---Prophets and teachers bar my way.

Tagore, by contrast, was a sophisticated Brahmin, a novelist, short story writer, satirist, playwright, painter, musician, and lyric poet, India's greatest poet. He was a renaissance man largely credited with introducing Indian culture to the West. He was lionized by Andre Gide and William Butler Yeats who wrote: "We fight and make money and fill our heads with politics—all dull things in the doing—while Mr. Tagore, like the Indian civilization itself, has been content to discover the soul and surrender himself to its spontaneity." He associated himself with the common man and examined "humble lives and their "small miseries."

A poet mustn't ever be
Like what he writes his verse on:
Let him not be entirely dense,
But eat and wash with honest sense,
And talk in simple prose, just like
A simple normal person.

His view of music was mystical: "Music fills the infinite between two souls." Much of his poetry was set to music. Two such poems became the national anthems of India and Bangladesh. Jana, Gana, Mana, the Indian anthem, builds to a crescendo that brings citizens to their feet, hands on hearts, and tears in eyes. The anthem's title means: Thou Art the Ruler of the Minds of All People. His most famous poetic creation was Gitanjali (Song Offerings), over 100 devotional poems based on ancient Hindu texts. Love is often the subject using imagery drawn from Nature. Imagine him in his Christ-like robes, long flowing beard, gentle gaze and this poem on his lips.

"The butterflies spread their sails on the sea of light. Lilies and jasmines surge up on the crest of the waves of light.

The light is shattered into gold on every cloud, my darling, and it scatters gems in profusion.

Mirth spreads from leaf to leaf, my darling, and gladness without measure. The heaven's river has drowned its banks and the flood of joy is abroad."

* * *

Between 1878 and 1932, Tagore set foot in more than thirty countries on five continents giving lectures and meeting with the likes of Albert Einstein, Robert Frost, Thomas Mann, Ezra Pound, George Bernard Shaw, and Butler Yeats.

Politically he was close to Gandhi imploring the British to leave, and even advised India's first president Jawaharlal Nehru. In his travels, he met Benito Mussolini. "Without any doubt he is a great personality." But he fumed about Il Duce's "fire-bath" of fascism and what it meant to "the immortal soul of Italy." When referring to the relationship between the British and Indians, Tagore spoke of a "dark chasm of aloofness." Today, we call it the arrogance of power...

Besides bequeathing India its national anthem, Tagore expressed his hopes for India, the largest democracy in the world. As the Nobel committee observed, Tagore's poetry gives expression to the spirit of a whole nation.

He appealed to the Lord for a country:

Where the mind is without fear and the head is held high;

Where knowledge is free;

Where the world has not been broken up into fragments by narrow domestic walls;

Where words come out from the depth of truth;

Where tireless striving stretches its arms towards perfection;

Where the clear stream of reason has not lost its way into the dreary desert sand of dead habit;

Where the mind is led forward by Thee into ever-widening thought and action

Into that heaven of freedom, my Father, let my country awake.

# Calcutta Karma

My friend Richard and I finished our business in Calcutta and decided to take the train home to Nepal where both of us were engaged as Peace Corps Volunteers. Well into our second year, we were seasoned enough to get along both in Hindi and Nepali. Adventurous by nature, Richard and I decided on a lark to travel to the India/Nepal border third class. Some would call it slumming; we called it "cultural immersion."

The overnight trip began in the Calcutta train station whose platforms were crowded with weary travelers and homeless men sleeping on the bare concrete, families sitting together for a meal of rice, lentils, and chapatis, an Indian bread. A legion of hawkers navigated carefully through the crowd peddling everything from spiced chai to betel nuts and little bidi cigars.

Our third-class tickets in hand, we boarded the Lucknow Express at dusk, a train that had seen better days during the British Raj. It was no surprise that we were the only sahibs in third class, but we were welcomed by the ragged, the infirm, and the lower castes. There were no passenger seats, only bunk beds stacked three high on either side of the car, and we took the topmost beds for the long night ride. Folks settled in for the night, some with animals, some with bad dreams.

Our iron horse sped along at a clickety-clack 60 miles-an-hour into a very black night with no electric lights. Unable to sleep much, I flicked my lighter to study my watch and noted three a.m. Snorts, snores and wheezes filled the cabin. Richard saw the light and whispered let's go into the vestibule for a smoke. We made our way into the enclosed space between cars where we could talk out loud without being heard and smoke some ganja, which Richard had thoughtfully purchased in a Calcutta bazaar. A few tokes and we began to appreciate the speed and rhythm of the train careening north and laugh about our silly adventure. Suddenly, Richard's jaw dropped, his eyes started, he pointed to the outside window. I looked behind me and gasped.

There hung a man upside down on the outside of the window with a frantic expression and frenzied finger pointing at the door handle. We sprang to the window, threw open the latch and hauled Ram Bahadur into the vestibule.

He was frightened, sooty, thirsty, hungry and grateful all at once.

Namaskar, Sahib! Shukriya! Shukryia! he blurted, his palms pressed together. We retrieved some water and shared our munchies. Realizing that we saved him from certain death, he felt compelled to tell us his story. He, like many other Indians, can't afford rail tickets and, as trains leave the station, they climb to the roof where they hitch a ride to towns along the way. Our fellow, whose name was Ram Bahadur Mukerjee, fell asleep on the roof. He awoke just as he was falling off the edge but managed to brake his descent into certain death by catching a guard rail with his feet and ankles thus explaining why he hung upside down. His middle name, Bahadur, means brave, and we thought, how apt…

The engine whistled just then as though to celebrate our victory over death. Richard wondered if Ram's rescue would increase our Karma. We passed the pipe around and laughed, almost hysterically.

# Hindu Holiday
# Calcutta Culture

Well into my two-year service in Peace Corps Nepal/India, I found myself once again in Calcutta (Kolkata today), this time for vacation, not business. I knew that the state of Bengal, of which Calcutta is capital, enjoyed the distinction of being India's cultural hub for music, dancing, painting, and poetry. It was also home to Rabindranath Tagore, India's poet laureate, and Ravi Shankar, the virtuoso sitar musician. I stood in awe of classical Indian culture and wanted to see and hear its best performers and artists up close. But I needed a guide and had just the person in mind – a Nepali girl friend who chose to live with her mother in the megapolis instead of a Nepali village. Her name was Mithu Kumari, about my age, and strikingly beautiful, which explained why she was a theatre actress who could also sing and dance, classic and Bollywood. Not a marquee name by any means, but a member of a troupe of actors that toured Nepali and Indian villages. We first met one evening after a light-hearted, thoroughly enjoyable outdoor performance on the edge of my little town, Gaur, Nepal. She must have followed someone's advice: *You ought to be on the stage!* She was quite exquisite dancing in her tightly wrapped red and gold sari, silky black hair, bejeweled necklace and gold nose ring. Mithu, educated in Kathmandu, could also speak a bit of English, about as well as I could speak Nepali. Between the two of us, we hit it off.

I de-trained at Calcutta's famous Howrah Railway Station, India's largest, a mammoth station that sees over a million travelers every day! I hailed a rickshaw to Mithu's address in a middle-class neighborhood. (There's something inherently repugnant about a man pulling another man through the teeming streets of Calcutta. But in the real world, it's hard to say *nahin* to a good fellow virtually begging for your business and knowing that his family depends on such fares). *Chalo!* Let's Go!

She met me at her apartment door and welcomed me with a happy face. She introduced me to her elegant mother who beamed when I said *Namaskar, Amma,* head bowed, palms together of course. She bade me sit and enjoy some Nepali chai, biscuits, veggie samosas, and a side of chutney, all servant-served. After a chat about things Nepali, Mithu insisted we leave in order to attend a private concert by a well-known local singer, Sandhya, whose connoisseur audience held her in high regard, much like the fans of jazz singer Nancy Wilson.

By the time we arrived at the open-air venue, the hour was late. The temperature had slouched into the comfortable 80s accompanied by an occasional zephyr. Torches cast a flickering light on the venue and kept the insects at bay. Jasmine incense wafted fragrantly, and the concert began.

Sandhya sat cross-legged on a platform in front of perhaps 100 Indians, Mithu, a Nepali, and me, an American. What could be better? Sitting next to a stunning beauty on a warm Bengali evening, secretly holding hands, and being moved by Sandhya's soul-stirring voice for over an hour? *Jai Hind!*

#

# Hindu Holiday, Part 2

Indians, for the most part, are very conservative when it comes to public behavior, especially displays of affection, double clutching or other allied activities. They certainly took note of a Westerner walking down a major Calcutta street in the company of an attractive Nepali starlet. Tired of the uncomfortable stares, we hailed a bicycle rickshaw built for two and careened toward the Great Eastern Hotel where Westerners frequent, meet and dine with their counterparts in government or business. After a spicy meal of chingri malai curry (prawns in coconut milk), a Bengali specialty, Mithu suggested we go to the zoo to see something very special and nowhere else to be found. My curiosity piqued, I hailed a rickshaw and off we went dodging enormous sacred cows along the way.

Arrived at the Calcutta Zoo & Zoological Garden, we paid the fifty rupees entrance fee and asked directions to the Big Cat cages. And there it was -- an albino Bengal tiger – all white with black stripes in a feline imitation of a zebra but looking just as fearsome as any other Bengal tiger. We then made the rounds of other cages, displays and gardens, so-called. The reptile garden allowed us to view cobras and kraits up-close, the latter a small brown snake more lethal than the cobra and the snake I nearly stepped on near my village in Nepal. Cobras are de-fanged so that the snake charmer will survive if he sways the wrong way – charming fellow.

Knowing my admiration of Mother Teresa, Mithu told the rickshaw walla to deliver us to her missionary. Chalo! He knew the address; everyone does. We disembarked at her famous, if ordinary, building where she and her missionaries looked after the destitute, the dying, the disabled, not to mention the helpless orphan. Before her death in 1997, she received the Nobel Peace Prize, the Bharat Ratna, India's highest civilian award, and over 120 other honors and accolades from around the world. After her death, she was canonized as a saint by Pope Francis. Mithu and I lingered long enough to read about her Catholic beginnings in Albania, not far from my relatives in southern Hungary. Mother Teresa's unlikely posting in Calcutta slums resulted in the even more unlikely establishment of a charitable mission, hospice, and leper colony. Unable to meet her, we made a modest donation and drew inspiration from her famous quotation: *What you spend years building may be destroyed overnight; build it anyway.* Sounds somewhat like Buddha's dictum: *If anything is worth doing, do it with all your heart.*

Mother Teresa

Back in my modest hotel lobby, I noticed several serious-looking Brahmins greet each other brotherly. I asked at reception who they might be and learned that they were high-caste Hindu philosophers who met regularly in a special hotel room. Given my total immersion in Hindu society for nearly two years, I jumped at the chance to clear up a few thorny theological issues and followed them down the hall. (As a long-time Unitarian, I also had a duty to investigate another's religion and internalize the best it had to offer.) Vide *The World's Religions* by Houston Smith.

I caught up with the Hindu gentlemen: *Namaskar Mahasaya*, and introduced myself and asked if a guest such as I would have the honor of joining them in theological discussions. All three of them responded with an enthusiastic welcome to an American volunteer with a caste name of Thapa, a step below the Brahmin caste. During my service, it became clear that a person without caste is unapproachable (not untouchable).  Removing our sandals, we entered the *special* room together.  Special indeed! The décor was dominated with conceptions and perceptions of Hindu mainstays: Ganesha, the plump and prosperous elephant god; the remover of obstacles, whose image can be found in every merchant's shop throughout India. More importantly, Lord Vishnu's more-or-less human avatar, divine Krishna, whose naughty behavior connects with devotees; behavior like baby Krishna stealing sweet butter on the sly, or, later in life, playing his flute while dallying with the pretty Gopis (milkmaids), then stealing their clothes while they bathed in the nude. Depicted on another wall, my favorite goddess, the beautiful Saraswati who sits on a lotus blossom or a white swan, depending on the artist, and plays the vinod, an ancient stringed instrument. She stands for knowledge and the classical arts.

# Hindu Holiday Part 3

Palms placed together prayerfully, incense lit, we sat on Kashmiri rugs more or less cross-legged. The brethren wore bright white dhotis, the ubiquitous wraparound for Hindu gentlemen, and, being Brahmins, they wore the sacred thread athwart their bare chests indicating that they had been twice-born, first into the flesh and again when initiated into their vocation a life devoted to sacred learning, not unlike a Catholic monk. After a bit of small talk about Nepal and its Hindu monarch, King Mahendra (I was able to tell them how many sugar cubes the King likes in his afternoon cup of chai – two; they chuckled), then we got down to business by chanting the well-known Hindu mantra, ÖM, the sound of Brahman, or God. Hindus believe that the creation of the universe began with the Sanskrit sound ÖM. And, in an astrophysical sense, they are right because we can now hear gravity.

\* \* \*

I threw them a soft ball to begin with:

*I know a Presbyterian minister who says that Hinduism has not weeded its theological garden. What do you suppose he meant? So many gods and goddesses?*

The eldest Brahmin spoke first. I could tell from the horizontal white lines on his forehead (smeared Sandalwood ash), that he chose to be a devotee of Shiva, the Cosmic Dancer, who brings the Black Age to a close in his role as the Destroyer to prepare the stage for Brahma, the Creator so that the cosmic dance can continue again and again and again…

# Lord Hanuman

*To begin with, there is no such a thing as Hinduism. That is a word coined by some Englishman. Now, I believe that your Presbyterian sect is several centuries old. They've hardly had time to stake out their garden, let alone weed it. We, on the other hand, have been reflecting, discoursing, interpreting, and writing about our beliefs for thousands of years, dating back to the Vedas, Upanishads, and Puranas, much like Jesus' Parables – received wisdom from the ancients. These gods and goddesses and their fantastic tales that so aggrieve your minister, are meant as symbols, not to be taken literally, but understood in their moral and ethical intent.*

The second Brahmin spoke up. I could tell by the three white lines smeared vertically on his forehead that he was a devotee of Vishnu, the Preserver.

*Mr. Thapa, you may have heard of the Ramayana, the Sanskrit story of Vishnu's avatar Rama. Rama, who rescues his beautiful wife, Sita, from the clutches of a demon king with the strong assistance of Hanuman, the flying monkey god. He symbolizes loyalty, selflessness, and duty. It is the story of righteousness and a tale of triumph over evil. Every Indian knows the story even if he is illiterate.* *

It was the turn of the third savant, a devotee of Brahma, the Creator, who, like devotees of Shiva the Destroyer, smears three white horizontal lines on his forehead but with an added all-seeing eye (bindu) between and slightly above his eye brows. This lens provides perception beyond ordinary sight, e.g., imagination and intuition.

*Perhaps you have heard of the Bhagavad Gita, Mr. Thapa. It is very old, over 5,000 years old. It has been passed down both by voice and in many written forms. Even your American, Oppenheiser (Oppenheimer, I interjected). Yes, Oppenheimer who quoted from the Gita moments after the first atomic explosion: Now I am become Death, the destroyer of worlds. And that is Shiva, the Destroyer.*

Then I pitched them a curveball:

*I understand about dharma, the right way of living, and how your actions in life, your karma, will determine your caste, higher or lower, when you are reincarnated or reborn. (Reincarnation is to the Hindu what the Resurrection is to a Christian.) This much I understand. What I don't understand is how this view can possibly be true when a baby or a toddler dies shortly after birth. Given the high rate of infant mortality here and in Nepal, what becomes of these dear little souls?*

I struck a nerve apparently because the three Brahmins began a fairly heated discussion among themselves in their native Bengali language. Perhaps they were weeding their garden. Their dispute was interrupted by a knock on the door. It was a servant of a lower caste bringing savory chai and vegetable samosas for our little band of seekers so hungry for knowledge and truth. Vegetarian of course.

*In the summer of 1988, sanitation workers across North India went on strike. Their demand was simple: they wanted the federal government to sponsor more episodes of a television serial based on the Indian epic Ramayana*

(Romance of Rama). More than eighty million Indians tuned in to every weekly episode. The government, faced with rising garbage mounds and the growing risk of epidemics, finally relented and millions of Indians celebrated.

# Hindu Holiday, Part 4

When we finished our afternoon repast, the same servant arrived with brass finger bowls so that we could purify ourselves, purity being a fundamental belief among caste Indians, a belief that goes well beyond mere cleanliness, soulfully speaking. Although this meeting took place over six decades ago, I can still remember feeling agreeably purified and decided to raise a subject I knew we could all agree on, namely, that the swastika you see in almost every northern Indian town is the Swastika Laundry sign. What gives? The eldest Brahmin knew I had pitched him a soft ball.

*We Indians all know that the swastika is an ancient Aryan religious symbol which was, How do you say? high-jack by the Nazis and used as propaganda to mean the victory of the Nazi German people over others. Today, like your four-leaf clover, it simply means Good Luck—The Good Luck Laundry, for example.*

Caste was among the other topics we discussed that late afternoon when the heat of the Indian sun begins to loosen its grip on the megacity of Calcutta. Caste, too, is losing its grip on modern-day Indian society in the largest democracy in the world. But democratic is not egalitarian as the caste system clearly demonstrates but with this caveat, no better explained than by Indianologist, Madeleine Biardeau:

*For the majority, caste is the sole means to social recognition. When a traveler arrives in a village, he states his name, caste and village so that everyone will know how to treat him. His position, however humble it may be, is his by rights. He feels at home in it, and has a sense of his inherent dignity, that of his caste. The Indian individual has no existence other than within and through his caste; outside it he is lost, no longer a man but a social outcaste (sic), a nonentity.*

I had learned to be especially cautious around orthodox Brahmins who have more to lose than other castes as poor villagers continue to migrate to the bustling cities in search of industrial employment among citizens of many castes, even untouchables, working side-by-side., shoulder to shoulder. Mindful of the fact that the caste system has maintained Indian civilization for thousands of years, I approached the subject carefully and with a little humor, a recommended technique before broaching a serious subject.

*Sri Sahibs, I am puzzled about certain aspects of caste. I have heard that the caste system was born in prehistoric times, its earliest manifestation having more to do with skin color than anything else. If that were true, I would be superior to you today which is a laugh, nahin? (The three Brahmins were light-brown complexioned.)*

They chuckled, thank Lord Shiva. One bemused Brahmin placed a meetha paan in his cheek and presented to the world a serene countenance. I couldn't tell if he experienced salivation or salvation.

(I too enjoyed the occasional after-dinner *meetha paan* with its sweet/ tangy taste due to a sophisticated blend of spices, chopped betel-nuts, and a smear of slaked lime, all wrapped up in a fresh betel leaf, a South Asian tradition for some 2,500 years.)

But I digress.

# Hindu Holiday, Part 5

The eldest Brahmin answered my speculation about skin color being the incipient basis for caste distinctions, and then he spoke wisely about caste.

*Perhaps that was true in the early eras when pale Aryans from the north eventually met dark peoples from the south, the Dravidians. We know that battles occurred. But as time passed, peace and order were imposed by the victors who became divine kings aided by Brahmin priests who could perform the rites and rituals associated with every life event: birth, initiation into adulthood, marriage, and death. Our gurus could read Sanskrit and interpret the ancient Vedas. They could invoke the gods to intervene at life's precarious moments or bless momentous events.*

*Essential to the kingdom were warriors to defend and administrators to govern. These are known as the kshatriya caste, like you, Mr. Thapa, because you work for His Majesty's government in Nepal. Kingdoms also need farmers and merchants and artists and their caste we call vaishyas. The fourth major caste is shudra, those who serve the other three castes.*

I deemed it diplomatic not to ask further questions about caste, especially the one about Mahatma Gandhi's anointment of untouchables, recasting them, as it were, calling them Harijans -- Children of God.

The hour was late; we decided to say farewell, but not before the eldest Brahmin said:

*With so many great religions worldwide, we know that there are many paths to the top of the mountain, the summit where Brahman reigns. Brahma, Vishnu and Shiva are his manifestation just as Father, Son, and Holy Ghost are for you. Good Bye, Mr. Makur Bahadur Thapa. We enjoyed your company and your excellent questions. Until we meet again (palms together; a slight bend at the waist). Namaskar.*

I felt blessed to have participated in an exchange about the Hindu world-view. (I sound like a Unitarian.) Respect and fellowship characterized our meeting. As dusk turned into another sultry evening, I mused on the ancients, the moderns, and their mutual devotion to the sacred scriptures replete with rules for living a pure life. The cardinal rule, the sacred, unspoken pledge among orthodox Brahmins, is this: "Always leave a place better than when you found it."

*"There's nothing wrong with you that reincarnation won't cure."*

—Jack E. Leonard

# The Lipnu Ladies

One of the first things you notice while wandering the medieval streets of Kathmandu or any other Nepali town are rows and rows of cow pies stuck up on the sides of buildings. They are drying in the sun for use as fuel for cooking. Wander farther and you'll soon witness a barefoot child following an enormous cow, a sacred cow, ready to pick up its dung and place it in a wicker basket to take home. Those were a few first impressions for a Peace Corps Volunteer just beginning to understand what lay ahead for the next two years.

When I finally arrived in my Himalayan hill village, Sindhuli Madhi, I was introduced to even more cow dung but for a different purpose. My thatched hut of clay and wattles made, boasted a clay floor with no furniture. The floor was badly cracked and pitted. The tea stall owner across the way knew just what to do and sent a courier to find the Lipnu Ladies.

Clad in colorful saris, two barefoot Nepali women soon arrived each carrying wicker baskets that contained mud and cow manure which, when mixed together, cancels any malodor. They mixed the two ingredients and began to lipnu, i.e., to smear. On hands and knees, the ladies applied the gaiko gobar to the entire floor and up the sides of the walls for a nice rounded baseboard. I paid the ladies and waited a few hours in the tea stall chatting with Monee Doj Rai, the retired Gurkha soldier. Look! a fresh new floor every two weeks. Now, I can lay down the Kashmiri rugs and the sleeping bag...Namaste!

# Taking Tea with a Rai Gurkha

While living in the little village of Sindhuli Madhi, Nepal, I had the great good fortune to meet and share tea with Munee Doj Rai, a retired Gurkha soldier. It was easy to do since he owned the tea stall across from my thatched-roof hut. His unusual name sounded a lot like $. But his last name derived from the Hindi raj. The Rai are people indigenous to eastern Nepal. Although they are influenced by Buddhism and Hinduism, they mostly worship Nature and Ancestors. They, along with the Limbu and Magar tribes, supplied the bulk of the Gurkha contingent to the British-Indian armies. Only the British were allowed to recruit soldiers in Nepal.

During one of our afternoon teas, Munee Doj recalled one operation during World War II about which he was particularly proud. It took place at night in an Italian village where German soldiers were asleep in their barracks. He and a comrade silenced two guards. Then Munee Doj, in stealth mode, crept into the middle of the barracks and decapitated a sleeping Kraut with a kukri, the famous Nepali knife that has the shape of a boomerang but with a handle and a razor-sharp inner edge. In no time, he was back outside with his mate, and together they stole into the night. When the Germans awoke and saw that one of their own and only one had been slaughtered during the night, the implication was clear, and troop morale fell to the floor. Ah, the good old days, said Munee Doj, and offered to refresh my cup of tea. Namaste!

# A Lofty Legacy

The recent death of Queen Elizabeth sparked many look-backs on her life and reign including one of her coronations, June 2nd, 1953. The photos were black and white, the young monarch was clad in smiles and surrounded by happy well-wishers. The reign of Queen Elizabeth II had begun. At the same time, on the other side of the planet, news broke that two men had just claimed the summit of Mt. Everest. Edmund Hillary of New Zealand and Tenzing Norgay, a Sherpa climber from Nepal had accomplished what others, dating back to 1922, had failed to do—conquer Sagarmatha, the mountain's Nepali name. Their achievement was broadcast around the world, and Britons hailed it as a good omen for the beginning of another Elizabethan era. The new queen learned of their achievement on June 1, the eve of her coronation. Later that year, she knighted Edmond, and he became Sir Edmund Hillary. Not being a Commonwealth member, Tenzing only received the British Empire Medal for "meritorious civil service worthy of recognition by the Crown" and the George Medal awarded for gallantry by a civilian.

Afterwards, Tenzing became a Nepali national hero and received many awards and lucrative opportunities. King Tribhuvan presented him with the Order of the Star of Nepal, 1st Class. The highest peak on the planet Pluto was named Tenzing Montes as well as a Himalayan peak in Nepal. He could neither read nor write but was heard to say: "It has been a long road…From a mountain porter to a wearer of a coat with rows of medals who is carried about in planes and worries about income taxes." He was famous for his flashing smile which I immediately noticed when I met him in Kathmandu and asked for his autograph and he obliged.

Tenzing and Edmund made a pact. They knew that the press would ask who ascended the summit first. So they pledged not to answer because the one couldn't have reached the top without the other. But when Hillary died in 2008, Tenzing allowed as how he had reached the summit first. No one contradicted him…especially when he flashed his signature grin.

# Mt. Everest is Sagarmatha

Tonight a gibbous moon is bright,
Directly overhead and stars
Illuminate a stygian night
And on the right, the planet Mars.

But muffled thunder greets the day,
And distant lightning looms o'erhead
Illuminating shades of gray
And darkling clouds a watershed.

Dawn breaks o'er mountain lake,
Thick with drizzle, darkening clouds.
Sodden, somber, some opaque,
Spread around like funeral shrouds.

A crown of stars rests lightly on
Great Sagarmatha's ancient brow,
And in the brightening rays of dawn,
He reigns as always, here and now.

'Neath scudding clouds and monsoon squalls,
We'll find the path as evening falls.

# Along the Way to Kathmandu

When walking from the Nepali/Indian border north to Kathmandu, you encounter some strange things, meet some unlikely creatures, and experience real fear for the first time in your life. Such was my trek north from the dusty border town of Gaur my first year in Peace Corps/Nepal. I had a nagging cough that required the help of the Peace Corps doctor in Kathmandu, and I had no other means of transport except a three or four day walk to Nepal's capital. Distances there are measured in the number of days it takes to walk no matter how the crow flies.

Nepal itself is about the size of Georgia—about 500 miles wide and one hundred miles, south to north, from a dusty, sea level border town to the snowy summit of Sagarmatha (Sanskrit for "Head of the Ocean"), what we call Mount Everest. There are essentially four distinct zones: The Terai or breadbasket of Nepal occupying the flat lands that border India; The jungle wherein Bengal tigers, wild elephants and one-horned rhinos still roam. The rugged, treacherous foothills leading to the even more treacherous, cold and snowy Himalayas. I would pass through three of those zones beginning in the Terai in a border town called Gaur where I lived my first year. There, I had access to better food than the hill villages but paid the price in hotter weather and the monsoon drenching that made for barefoot, muddy walks to Ram Bahadur's little thatch-roofed restaurant for rice, spicy lentils, curried tomatoes, and cauliflower—delicious. "More rice, please."

Back in my two rooms, I lit the kerosene lamp and opened to my bookmark *The Dubliners* by Joyce. Sometimes my eyes would flicker in sync with the flames. Lokalal, a minor government official, might arrive, a friendly fellow a little older than I and, importantly, spoke a good deal of English. I told him once to come over because a care package from mother arrived at last, and we should open it together. Lokalal had the foresight to bring some ganja because mother's box probably contained some candy bars, soup, and Kool-Aid, which nicely masked the taste of the iodine we had to use before drinking the water. Thank you, Mom.

Next morning, I caught a Nepali-owned Russian jeep going north near Lumbini where Buddha was born in 563 BC. The road north was deeply rutted from the large wooden wheels of ox-carts carrying all manner of goods to villages along the way. By the time we reached the jungle, I was thankful to leave the jeep and the two-hour bumpy ride we had to endure. Besides my tingling spine, the only lasting memory of the trip was a paraplegic man, his trunk somehow attached to a board shuffling along the dusty shoulder. He propelled himself by reaching out ahead with his fists planted firmly in the dust, and then pulling his body forward another two feet or so. The temperature was only 101.

The jungle is very quiet in the morning as the sun starts hitting the trees, dappled light coming to the jungle floor. Very cool. I set off alone, my Kelty backpack secure with sleeping bag firmly in place. Besides the raucous bird cries, only monkey chatter filled the tree tops. Hearing them, I thought of Hanuman, the monkey god of Sanskrit lore and legend who represents courage, self-control, faithful selfless service. He makes his cameo appearance in the Ramayana circa 500 BCE as the faithful servant of Rama the son of Vishnu. Because of his importance as a figure of righteousness, we can only imagine the Hindu reaction to the proposal by the Archbishop of India some years ago. He pontificated: "The solution to hunger in India is simple. Kill all the monkeys eating the food that properly belongs to mankind." I mused on how that ancient monkey god manifests himself in the lives of people today whose history is older than that of the Chinese, let alone Greek and Roman ways.

Wending my way along a narrow jungle path, I suddenly emerged in a clearing whose outstanding feature was a stand of wild bamboo that I had never seen before, especially one with a leafy crown. I approached and grasped one of the thicker stalks when instantly a flock of bright green parrots exploded from the crown startled and not happy judging from their collective squawks and screeches. The flock flew; I trekked, a little shaken, due north until I came to a dirt road in the jungle. I decided to follow it east. As I was walking along admiring the massive jungle on either side, I caught something in my peripheral vision. I was being stalked. His head was down, his eyes fixed, and his long tail in the upright position. I quickened my pace as my mind raced for safety. I could see the headline: "PCV Mauled by Bengal Tiger in Nepal Jungle." For the first time in my life, I felt real fear and began to panic as the creature came closer. Just as I was about to make a run for it, I had one more look and realized it wasn't a tiger after all but a large adult monkey hoping to cadge some food. I laughed with joy, almost hysterically. I named him Hanuman. Buddhists name him Maya (illusion).

My next stop was a village where a work crew of Russians was engaged in the construction of the road I had just traveled. A Nepali official greeted me and asked if I wanted to meet the crew. Sure. As soon as the Rooskies learned my nationality, they began bragging in loud broken English how their weightlifters took home the Olympic gold and silver while the Amerikanskies took home nothing. Raucous laughter. I didn't argue, but I turned to the official and asked in Nepali where the road would go. "As far east as possible." The Russians couldn't speak Nepali, and it definitely made an impression when they heard us conversing. The Nepali official took note. (It's true; we're in serious competition with Russia in developing countries. Just ask our Ambassador to Nepal at the time, Claire Laise, the wife of the U.S. Ambassador to Vietnam, Ellsworth Bunker.)

"Where is a tea stall where I can rest and eat something before continuing my journey?" Since dusk was nearly upon us, he suggested I stay the night on the porch of the local judge. Gratefully, I took his advice, found the house, and made myself known. The judge was out of town but his wife and their servants would feed me and make me comfortable on the porch as the starry night began to sparkle (chilli-milli) unlike bright electric light. A clear vision claimed my attention and imagination as I lay in my sleeping bag looking up. Starry-eyed, I fell into a sound sleep.

Next morning, after a delicious breakfast of rice, lentils, curried squash and chai, I exited the jungle and began trekking the foothills of the great Himalayas. Its snow melt meant cold water and raging rivers. I soon heard the roar of one and walked off the beaten path to marvel at it. Massive waves of frothy brown water hurled down a steep river bed toward the sacred Ganges. *At last! something worthy of the word awesome.* On my way back to the path, through tall wheat-like grass, I came face to face with a Shiva linga—the Sanskrit word for sign or symbol. "A gateway to the beyond." That's the Shiva temple version. But everyone knows that it's also a phallic symbol and has been for thousands of years. I put my hand out and touched the ancient, chest-high, middle-of-nowhere stone phallus (*Hey Bro*). I recalled reading somewhere that village women who had problems conceiving or simply wished to be more fertile, would scrape off a tiny bit of linga stone, a scratch really, mix it with sacred cow milk and oregano—the spice of life— and swallow it prayerfully. Where you find a linga, a yoni can't be far off. I looked closely at the linga's base, cleared the dead grass debris and, Voila!, a yoni, the female symbol—in this case an oval-shaped stone whose base represents the Supreme Power that holds the universe within it. Of course women already knew that.

My cough worsened, and I struggled at times to climb the steep stone staircases whose steps were worn and polished from a million Nepali feet over the centuries. Remote Himalayan hill country has bred a hardy people who have weathered every heat wave or monster monsoon for a thousand years or more. They are strong (a hundred pounds are nothing when you wear a head strap); sturdy (carriers typically have calves the size of bowling pins); reliable (for the most part); hearty (except when they're angry).

I finally stopped in a tiny hill village exhausted and hungry. "Please bring me some supper." I waited for a very long time. An emaciated courier finally brought me one hard-boiled egg, rice, and gundruk, a fermented leafy green vegetable (spinach or mustard greens, radish and cauliflower leaves) that originated in Nepal. It's dark brown and sour, utterly unique, and rather disgusting on first bite. But, like the Nepalese, you make due, a key concept in the Peace Corps.

The next day's trek included a river fording that barely succeeded against a strong current. The next hilltop afforded magnificent views of the terraced rice paddies marching down the hillsides. The heat, the sweat, the load and the cough began to wear me out. I was grateful therefore to arrive at a small path-side tea stall that also served chang, the Nepali rice beer. It was contained in a large clay jar with a woven straw lid. Fermentation made the beer cold. It was the most refreshing drink served me in Nepal. Onward!

As I arrived in the Kathmandu valley, I came to a path with hedge rows on either side. As I approached, small brown leeches sensed my blood and reached out to latch on my body, it didn't matter where. Their anti-coagulant went to work on my ankles, and I began to bleed. A lit cigarette butt applied to their disgusting butts released their hold and dropped off. Locals hate leeches because they attach to the inside of their cattle's throats and cause internal bleeding that can actually kill the cow and the bull. I addressed my wounds with first aid bandages and struggled on into the city as darkness fell. I found the house of a fellow PCV and knocked on his door. His girlfriend opened it, and I collapsed to the floor.

The next day, after a deep sleep, I was carried to the doctor's office in a rickshaw. The doctor didn't take long to diagnose my problem: double pneumonia. Welcome to Nepal. Namaste.

# Tea for Me but Not for Thee— A Liberal's View

Tea claims no political affiliation, does it? You could be a Marxist or a MAGA man and still enjoy a cup of tea. They might differ on their choice of blend with vague political implications – green teas from southern China vs. black teas from the Indian state of Assam. Thousands of variations are enjoyed worldwide every day.

But what about the 18th century days of the British Raj when there was no Indian tea? As tea-drinking became fashionable in English society (Earl Grey especially), Brits got tired of spending silver for Chinese tea and wondered why they couldn't harvest tea leaves in their own India. They even sent a secret agent into China to smuggle tea plants, plants that ultimately failed to take root in Himalayan soil. This agricultural failure left the East Indian Company (EIC) and its shareholders in London scratching their heads. Quite by accident, a solution presented itself. Colonials and English investors awoke one morning to the news that an adventurous Scotsman named Robert Bruce, while exploring the remote jungles of Assam, an Indian state close to China, had discovered an indigenous tea that indigenous tribes had been drinking for centuries. Best of all, it made a better brew than the Chinese blends. (Was it Prime Minister Rajiv Gandhi who quipped, "If the tea that American revolutionaries tossed into Boston Bay had come from Assam instead Amoy, they might have thought of a less wasteful method of protest.") English housewives found the black tea more palatable for afternoon tea and crumpets; more sociable, you might say.

English colonials leapt to the challenge, converting whole jungles to tea plantations, destroying acres of wildlife habitat in the process. Indian laborers were paid a pittance for plucking and processing tea leaves in the jungle-hot sun all day.* The British grew tea for themselves, not for the locals. But when the Great Depression of the 1930s grew nigh and the market sagged, the Brits had the bright idea of selling their produce to the Indians who, it just so happened, were delighted and fell in love with their own beverage. Imagine, Indians drinking Indian tea! An aggressive marketing campaign blanketed India and ran parallel with the rising Indian Independence Movement. It didn't take long for chai to become the national drink. Today, more Indians drink black tea than the rest of the world combined. Early in my tour, I asked for coffee, and the waiter brought me a cup of hot water and a jar of Sanka. Thereafter, I had the pleasure of becoming a fan of Nepali spiced chai.

These revelations and more were prompted by a question I asked my surrogate father, Babu, one evening as we sat on the porch drinking Nepali chai infused with water buffalo milk and spices.

"Babuji, would you consider yourself a liberal or, like most other Brahmins, a conservative?"

He didn't hesitate. "A liberal."

And to prove it, he recalled a time 20 years before when an Indian tea sampler walked into town to coax folks to try the new Indian drink. Well, young Babu was the only one in Gaur to step forward for a sample sip, thereby defining him as a liberal. Thus does one tea claim a political affiliation!

*Appalling conditions included (and still do) cobra and pit viper snake bites.

# When Sharing Tales With Nepalese

When sharing tales with Nepalese,
I wander back in time
To my old village in Nepal
Where I did once abide.

Sindhuli Madhi was its name,
A Himalayan site:
With Annapurna on the left,
And Everest on the right.

Thatched roof adorned my village hut,
While mud and cow dung formed the floor,
And mud and wattle were its walls.
No sense to lock the door.

My lanterns fed with kerosene
Provided reading light,
And I had water from our stream
To bathe in every night.

The milk of water buffalo
To froth my tea each morn;
Good chai from tea stalls down below
And by my bearer borne.
Sir Adhikari was his name
Just eighteen years of age,
A Hindu Brahmin, he became
My guide and cook and sage.

He cooked me rice and lentil soup,
Spiced vegetables a treat;
The fish he found in our bazaar
Were barely fit to eat.

Our hardships though were small indeed
Compared to village ways;
The men were yoked to ox and plow
The same as ancient days.

When looking out our window gap,
One cloudy afternoon,
We saw a body borne aloft
Before the great monsoon.

The mourning family bore the corpse
And placed it on a pyre
Beside the rushing river shore,
And set their son on fire.

We watched the smoke ascend like shrouds
We watched the Hindu priest,
We watched the billows reach the clouds
And with them the deceased.

These memories oft return to me,
Both pleasant and profound,
When I sit down with Nepalese
On this my native ground.

Mourners

A dear deceased son to the funeral pyre

# The Far Side of Earth, The Dark Side of the Moon

When she first saw me, the jar of water on her head almost fell into the dusty road.

Recovering her balance if not her composure, she heard me say *Namaste* but rapidly walked away behind a hut.

After a long day's trek starting in Pokhara that morning, I was covered in sweat and dust, and my Kelty Pack felt heavier than usual. I was pretty sure that I had taken a wrong turn early on and didn't even know the name of the village I had just stumbled into. As I un-shouldered my pack, a gentleman about sixty made his appearance wearing a lungi wrap-around, T-shirt and a special Nepali hat called a topi to indicate he was a local official, probably the mayor. I put my palms together and said *Namaskar Hazoor*, the honorific title of respect I used often during my two years in Peace Corps/Nepal. The look on his face told me that he couldn't believe his ears let alone his eyes because, as I found out later, I was the first Westerner ever to enter his village.

"Khasto hunchha, Hazoor?" I asked. He said he was just fine and then began a short conversation to find out who I was and why I had arrived in his village. First, sir, may I trouble you for some water? He barked an order and in no time I had a tumbler of pure Himalayan-fed water. I told the mayor, Sri Ram Adhikari Baun, that I was an American but worked for His Majesty's Government in Kathmandu, and I came to find out about development programs in his village, a village that had no electricity or running water outside the rambling river that ran nearby. Then I told him my Nepali name, Makur Bahadur Thapa -- Brave Jupiter of the Thapa caste, one step down from the mayor's Brahmin caste. The perfect host, he barked an order, and I thought I heard: *Slaughter the Goat!* I was right. We would feast tonight.

I was led to the mayor's home with a large porch and settled there to take a rest after my all day trek up ancient stone steps. I was now in an orthodox Hindu village whose residents had never seen anyone like me. My Nepali name, Makur Bahadur Thapa, had served me well over the past two years. The caste name, Thapa, fit my job description as a government worker, and I was treated with respect. I did not mention the words Peace Corps. It was an unfortunate name from the start. The soldiers who guarded our Embassy in Kathmandu were Marines. Since the Nepali dictionary defined Corps as a military unit, Peace Corps became an instant oxymoron and instantly fed into the narrative that Peace Corps was simply another name for CIA. No, I'm just an ordinary American who came to help out and let it go at that. My reveries were interrupted by an invite to dinner. As the sun was settling into a pure perfect mountain night, I was led to a large home where the village elders, sitting cross-legged around a glowing warm fire pit, greeted me sincerely, almost reverently, with deep bows and friendly expressions. What would the evening bring?

Since our only light was firelight and a few sooty kerosene lanterns, I couldn't get a clear view of the women in the dark recesses cooking the meal. I could only smell their creations. Soon a plate arrived with squares of hot goat meat, skin intact, bite size. The elders prevailed on me to try their delicacy. As I lifted the first bite to my mouth, I couldn't help notice that the animal's fur hadn't been completely burned off, and I was about to sink my teeth into a charred stubble or two. Well, it was tasty enough but one of those delicacies that gets bigger the more you chew it. I sent my compliments to the chefs back there in the smoke-filled recess which made them all laugh. I took another sip of *rakshi*, a powerful drink made from fermented millet that all but cancelled the taste of stubbled goat skin. After a wonderful meal of rice, lentils, spicy stewed tomatoes, curried pumpkin and sizzling goat meat all served on banana leaves, we got down to business. It was summer, 1969. Neil Armstrong and Buzz Aldrin had just stepped onto the moon. My hosts had heard about it from the transistor radio His Majesty's Government had given to every village leader.

Bellies full of curry and *rakshi*, they began to ask questions. I begged them to slow down. "Is it true that Americans flew to the moon and settled there?" Well yes, Sri Armstrong and Sri Aldrin are both Americans, but they didn't settle; they flew back home. There was a long pause. Shadows flickered on the mud-dung walls. Mountain chills set in. The eldest of the elderly finally spoke up to say that their village was not in favor of such a flight because their goddess Saraswati abides on the moon, and they didn't want her tranquility disturbed. I knew that Saraswati was the goddess of music, poetry and everything that flows. I let the seriousness of their grievance sink in. I knew that a white lie was necessary, and I suddenly found myself saying, "You need not worry. The control center knows where Saraswati abides. And that is why they landed on the opposite side of the moon." The proverbial pregnant pause followed. I took a sip of *rakshi* and looked the old one in the eye. He suddenly smiled with an expression of good will and understanding. The mood lightened and thereby encouraged another elder to ask, "How many rupees did it cost?" I had read somewhere that the Apollo mission cost nearly a billion dollars, but my Nepali vocabulary was not up to the task. "What is the most expensive thing in your village?" I asked. A water buffalo at 1200 rupees a head. Rounding up for cost overruns, I donned a serious expression and said, "About 25 million water buffalo." The Nepalese don't say Wow! when amazed, nor do they emit a low whistle. In unison, the village elders said Bhaprebhop!

And that's how the evening ended. We bade each other a fond good night, and I retired to my porch and sleeping bag for a long look at the night sky brilliant with stars and the moon unimpeded by electric lights. Suddenly I thought of Brigadoon, the bewitching Scottish village appearing only once in awhile but, in my case, appearing once in a lifetime…

Raj and I lived on the second floor; kitchen below.
This hut was a duplex and here are my neighbors.l

Two of my neighbors Up close and personal

# The Rana Ruse

It's not often that one comes into contact with a member of a real dynasty, one that does not include Joan Collins. Perhaps you shook the hand of a Kennedy or a Bush or a Yankee. In my case, I met and broke biscuits with members of the Rana dynasty that ruled the Kingdom of Nepal from 1846 to 1951 when the Shah monarchy was restored. The Ranas are very wealthy, well educated and still engaged in governing the country as I soon found out at the beginning of my two-year service in Peace Corps/Nepal. Dron Shumsher Rana ruled the District where I lived for a year. He lived in a country palace whose fireplace was large enough to roast a whole goat and whose Bengal tiger skin sprawled comfortably on the hearth while staring at me with hungry eyes. The Rana dynasty included prime ministers and maharajas and autocrats known for their iron-fisted rule. My Rana was domineering, arrogant, and authoritarian. He owned a dozen servants; he owned a Russian jeep; he owned several elephants and their mahouts; and he made life-altering decisions every week when presented with petitions from supplicant villagers. His authority was recognized as final.

* * *

Nearing the end of my two-year service, I spent my last week wandering around Kathmandu visiting familiar sites, Peace Corps friends, and Nepali families. During one such visit, I was introduced to Chandra Bahadur Rana who, after a friendly talk, invited me for afternoon tea at the main Rana palace. Confident that their digs were more resplendent than my thatch-roofed hut, I readily accepted.

I arrived on time, looking sharp in my Nepali cap and sporting a pin featuring King Mahendra. The palace façade is grandiose and makes an immediate impression of opulence. Its architecture and interior were meant to duplicate both the look and the furnishings of the Palace of Versailles. Landscaped grounds and manicured gardens surround the elegant edifice.

I was made welcome and, palms together, replied in the best formal Nepali I could muster (*Namaskar Hajur!*) and engaged in small talk with the three aristocratic gentlemen who greeted me. While waiting for chai and biscuits, I asked if I might admire the details of the drawing room like the heavy silk drapery, the tiger skin and large Kashmiri rugs on marble floors, the overstuffed leather armchairs featuring elegantly embroidered antimacassars. Rana knickknacks included enormous elephant tusks, Venetian glass, Japanese vases, gilt mirrors, crystal chandeliers, and, "Oh! Aren't these Dutch oil paintings!?"

"Yes and the portraits are of Ranas who ruled the kingdom for over a hundred years. That one is Fakht Simha Rānā who had a son named Rāma Simha Rānā..."

They were all uniformed, carrying swords and bearing rows of medals, stern epaulets overseen by plumed crowns, bordered by gilded frames.

At that moment, the Nepali chai (hidden beneath a tea cozy), bickies, and various condiments arrived on Chinese china borne by impeccable servants. There were smiles all around. The chit chat paused long enough to savor the curried pumpkin, mango pickle, and perfect tea. Just as the plates were being cleared, a door I hadn't noticed opened and a vision appeared. She was the loveliest young woman I had seen during my two years in Nepal. Lustrous black hair cascaded down her pure white sari. She came to me and introduced herself with a gentle voice and angel's face.

"I am Prithi Narayan Rana. And you have a Nepali name my uncle tells me: Makur Bahadur Thapa. Brave Jupiter of the same caste as the Rana's: Thapa."

So smitten with her grace and beauty, I didn't notice that the three gentlemen had quietly disappeared from the drawing room leaving Prithi and me alone. She took my hand and bade me follow her through a small door that led to a dark spiral staircase. We ascended the narrow stairwell in close contact, her perfume a jasmine garden. Midway, she stopped, embraced me, and planted a charming kiss on my welcoming lips. But just as heaven was opening its gates, her hand grasped mine and guided it to her crotch. Therein, taking up space, was a turgid member not of her sex. He moaned; I fled and boarded the next plane home. The Rana Ruse was complete.

# Snapshots

If you're ever invited to play golf at the New Delhi Country Club, the first thing you notice is that each tee-box stands in the shadow of an ancient mausoleum. And don't be alarmed by the two servants standing in the middle of the first fairway waiting for your first drive. Your host, the son of the Indian Ambassador to America, sees your quizzical expression and quickly explains that the "boys" are there to protect your new white Titleist from being snatched by monkeys watching intently from nearby trees.

\* \* \*

Spinning a line of Buddhist prayer wheels in Kathmandu your first week in town is very cool and done with the same wrist action as skittering a stick along the ribs of an old radiator. Inside each wheel is a tightly rolled scroll containing a mantra or a sacred symbol or a prayer.

Keep spinning, Sahib, but slowly. Each revolution is like a prayer to the world. ***Om Mani Padme Hum***.

Animal sacrifices to various gods, especially Kali who demands a blood sacrifice, are not uncommon in Nepal's hill districts and even in Kathmandu. Chickens are popular along with rice, various fruits, flowers and yoghurt. The most dramatic sacrifice is that of the water buffalo. Only one stroke of the khukuri blade beheads the creature, and all the blood gushes into a huge copper basin for use in foods and god knows what else. Ignore rumors of child sacrifices; that was long ago.

Know that when you play chess with a native, you will probably lose. Chess was invented in India. Other things invented in India include: the numeral Zero without which modern mathematics is, well, stumped. And don't forget the decimal system we use today. Meet the genius mathematicians, Aryabhata, and his inspired follower, Brahmagupta who first recognized Zero as an actual number, not just a place holder.

\* \* \*

After dinner in a village restaurant, you take a toothpick by reaching up on your way out to pluck a straw from the thatch roof overhang. Anise seeds are the preferred after dinner mint.

\* \* \*

The Swiss taught the Nepalese how to make cheese. The water buffalo milk adds an extra sharp dimension. Local mice are thrilled.

\* \* \*

Buddhists worldwide know that Buddha attained enlightenment while meditating beneath the bodhi tree in northern India. What they don't know is what goes on around the bodhi tree at nighttime. I do because an ancient, immense bodhi grew just across the way from my thatched hut. The old tree had to be proud of its prominent above-ground roots whose folds provided places to sleep for the exhausted porters carrying salt, kerosene, and other staples to remote villages. As the moon appears, they settle in, men on one side of the wise bodhi, women on the other, and they flirt by singing charming little insults and suggestive stanzas directed to anyone on the opposite side of the tree.

"Don't walk away from me like that with your hips swinging (dhaliki -dhaliki). You might stir certain embers."

"It would be easy to walk away from a slow porter like you, darling."

"If only your eyes were as pretty as your smile, you'd look my way."

Et cetera, until they fall into dreamland, soon to wake up and continue trekking with ungodly loads.

When you first see it, on Kathmandu's Main Street no less, you're half shocked, half touched. You can tell from his bureaucratic uniform that he's a high-ranking official, and there he his bending down on the sidewalk, pedestrians streaming by, and touching his forehead to the bare feet of his guru wrapped in a white dhoti, bare-chested -- respect personified. Guru touches the former student on the head and bids him stand to receive a Namaskar, a blessing, and probably an attaboy.

When winter arrived and brought welcome relief from the heat, it sometimes turned the evenings downright cold. My fellow Volunteers and I would walk down the dusty road, flashlights in hand, to our favorite little restaurant with no signage, no menus or utensils, but a fine reputation. The owner and his sous-chef served but one entrée – *dal, bhat, tarkari* – lentils, rice and vegetables,  the former and latter being highly spiced and serving as a countervailing force to the cold night air wafting through the windows, doors, and cracks. The banana leaves were laid, monsoon water served, and heaping mounds of rice ladled onto each leaf. We experienced a near-spiritual high when we thrust our frigid fingers into the mound of steaming rice and just let them stay there for a while. Haute cuisine, Nepali style. Ah. Chai with water buffalo milk.

My helper's name was Ishwar Raja Adhikari Baun. I found him one day on a nearby trail walking alone, looking for work. He had just turned 18; I asked him to be my helper. He turned out to be a wonderful fellow who knew how to cook, as most Brahmins do because they won't eat food prepared by one of lower caste. A rough translation of his name:  Ishwar means, among other things, Supreme Self; Raja means King; Adhikari means officer; and

Baun is the Sanskrit word for Brahmin. I called him Raj and left him all my gear when I left Sindhuli Madi.

* * *

Hill Nepalis would not, could not believe that our only black Volunteer, Bill Nance, was an American. He spent two years trying to convince them. But they sure liked him and admired his work as an overseer. So did we all.

Rugged individualists, as we know and esteem them in the West, don't exist in Nepal; at least I didn't meet or see any. Togetherness is the custom and the rule. Even in a big house, family members crowd into one room. Privacy as a concept doesn't exist. This need -- never to be alone -- sometimes causes tragic incidents. We all heard about suspension bridges collapsing because porters wouldn't cross alone but needed to cross close together. The bridge couldn't withstand their combined weight, snapping a cable and sending them to their deaths on the rocky crags below, all because they wouldn't cross solo.

* * *

As I was musing on Maya at dusk and noticing a snake ahead on the path, I saw an elderly Indian woman approach. She walked right by the snake ignoring it, and I realized it was but a stick in the road. She was wrapped in a work-a-day sari, bare foot, and carrying a basket on her head. She eyed me suspiciously; I said Namaste, palms together, respectful bow. She wanted to talk when I told her I was an American. With one hand on her basket and the other one pointed at me, she had a crossy-wossy demeanor and was aching to ask a question: "Is it true that you eat cows in your country, that you eat your mother?" She was referring of course to the sacred cows of India. Coming from the Beef State I said "Yes we do, but I don't while working in India. Besides, we would rather have our mothers inside of us than wandering in the fields or lying in the middle of the dusty road." Needless to say, after her snort of derision, I didn't tell her that the owners of Omaha Steaks International were family friends.

* * *

If you're in Old Delhi one day and wander into a Male Only public bath, knowing you'll be the only Westerner there, how do you address the gentlemen wrapped in Turkish towels and shod in flip-flops?  Some are Muslims, most are Hindus.  Well, if you're a veteran Volunteer, you watch closely:  Muslims wash from the hands up to the elbows; Hindus, from the elbows down to the finger tips.  It's all in the details.

# Notes from Nepal

When I served in Peace Corps/Nepal from 1967 to 1969, I never imagined that I would live amongst some of the nicest, most gentle people I had ever met. As my language ability improved, the walls almost disappeared, and I found myself talking to a gentleman half a world away, in his language, laughing at his tall tales or clearing up the misconception that he could walk to America just like he walked anywhere in landlocked Nepal. I treasure the name they gave me: Makur Bahadur Thapa—Brave Jupiter of the Thapa caste. Thapa because I worked for His Majesty's government. Only Brahmins were my betters.

I considered myself a very lucky man to have lived in Sindhuli Madi, about a three day trek to Kathmandu, up and down steep Himalayan foothills. The majestic Himalayan range dwarfs the Alps or the Rockies. The green terraced paddy fields skip down the foothills. The monstrous monsoon that waters those paddies also drowns and dislocates thousands of villagers every year.

After the devastating earthquakes in 2015, thousands lay dead, tens of thousands wounded, hundreds of thousands homeless. Clean water, food, medicines and tents were in short supply. Epidemic diseases loomed. Ancient palaces and sacred places destroyed, pagoda temples, Hindu and Buddhist shrines -- edifices I remember well-- became rubble.

I was relieved to find alive and uninjured my friend, Bell Prasaad Shrestha, the former mayor of Dhulikhel, about two hours east of Kathmandu Valley up on the rim. The hospital that B.P. built overflowed with the injured. Bodies were being stacked one on the other. I could just imagine the funeral pyres alight that week. It's the way of both Hindus and Buddists. My poem recounts the one I saw:

When looking out our window gap,
One cloudy afternoon,
We saw a body borne aloft
Before the great monsoon.

The grieving family bore the corpse
And placed it on a pyre,
Beside the rushing river shore,
And set their son on fire.

We watched the smoke ascend like shrouds
We watched the Hindu priest,
We watched the billows reach the clouds
And with them the deceased.

What a terrible tragedy for a country with the fewest resources to weather the ordeal. It's the injured and homeless of course who will suffer most…Thank God for the Red Cross, CARE, OXFAM, Catholic Relief Services, UNICEF and other worthy organizations. These good people deserve our gratitude and assistance. To Nepalis I send hope and prayer and money. Namaste mero sathi haru…goodbye, my friends

# Afterword

For how many years have we heard the refrain: "The world is getting smaller?"

After my years living abroad, I contend that the world is getting larger, at least through the Peace Corps lens. It's one thing to highlight the advances in telecommunications and transportation -- advances that allow us to communicate instantly or travel halfway around the globe in a day or so in order to scale a Himalayan peak. But it's quite another experience to live for two years in a Nepali village to lend a hand and project something other than the complaining, demanding tourist, say, or a proselytizer on a mission to tell the gospel truth. Without going completely native, Nepal Volunteers learned the language; learned to live without indoor plumbing or electricity; learned to eat local fresh food including the skin and every internal organ of the goat. We attended and even participated in Hindu and Buddhist festivals wearing local garb, and sometimes fell sick from the same bugs as any villager. It was easy to empathize. As we began to fall in with village ways and diurnal rhythms and learned the lay of the land, we realized how large the world really is, no matter how it shrinks in travel time or internet.

I had the unique experience of living on the India/Nepal border one year and in a Nepali hill village the next year. Border Nepalese looked and acted so much like Indo-Aryans that it was sometimes hard to see any difference. But the Hill Nepalese are a different breed, as they say. Ethnographers call them indigenous tribal Peoples, many with Mongoloid features: the Magars, the Rai, the Tamang and, perhaps most famous, besides the Sherpas, the fierce Gurkha soldiers who stymied the advances of British brigades and left Nepal an independent Kingdom, landlocked, but virtually unaffected by the near 200 years of Rule Britannia throughout most of India. Geopolitically speaking, Nepal's topography saved it from the looting and pillage that left India in the poverty-stricken condition I witnessed and you can still see in many areas today, despite heroic (and nuclear) efforts to catch up to modern states. Yes, Nepal is poor, too, but in a different way, a way that has more to do with terrain and climate than with rapacious British administrators, armies, and merchants. No wonder Brits called India the Jewel of the Crown.

Privately, Nepalis told me that they don't much like the Indians (traders or tourists and merchants) who try to take advantage of them in their reduced circumstances, especially after the earthquakes of 2015. They think New Delhi's power elite are overbearing, arrogant, and paternal to their hillbilly brothers. Things will not change much as long as India controls port cities like Calcutta that allow Nepali goods to enter global markets.

Today, a quarter of a million Americans identify themselves as Nepalese, the fastest growing Asian American population. So, if you identify a Nepali in your neck of the woods, say ***Namaste*** and get to know a delightful newcomer.

# Glossary

*amma*---Mother. Our kids say mamma.

*baba*---Father. Ours say dada.

*baksheesh*---The coins (paisa) that a beggar asks for with his hand out and a stricken expression. It can also be a bribe.

*bhajan*---Hindi devotional songs from ancient to Bollywood.

*bidi*---a mini-cigar filled with tobacco, wrapped in a special leaf, and tied together with a colorful thread. For those who can't afford cigarettes.

*bojan*---Distinctive Indian cuisine -- korma, vindaloo, tandoori, naan, etc.

*chia pasals*---Nepali tea stalls for trekker rest and refreshment.

*chillum*---The pipe used to smoke ganja.

*dal, bhat, tarakari*---lentils, rice, vegetables eaten twice a day with snacks in between.

*dhanyabad*---Thank you.

*dhobi*---The Nepali laundry woman. Rocks, not Tide, clean clear through but shorten the garment's life.

*dhoti*---Male only wrap-around and through the legs like Gandhi wore.

*ganja*---Marijuana, a Nepali cash crop for thousands of years.

*ghungroos*---Ankle bells worn by a classical dancer.

*gundruk*---A vegetable made by fermenting the leafy greens of mustard, carrots, and spinach originated in Nepal and foul-tasting on first bite...

*khukuri*---The famous Gurkha knife.

*lingam*---Sanskrit meaning sign or mark. A prominent representation (often in stone) of the erect male organ, an ancient symbol of Lord Shiva's virility and found all over Nepal and India. And where there's a turgid member, look for the nearby yoni or female representation.

*lota*--A small brass vessel of water, one of Nepal's toiletries instead of TP. No TP, Sahib.

*lungi*---Traditional Nepali/Indian garment – a colorful wrap-around (the waist down) worn day or night by men and women. Different from dhoti.

*mritasanjivani*—Ayurvedic medicine. Sanskrit meaning "to be taken at the point of death." "I'll take two, please."

*Namaskar*---The formal greeting reserved for V.I.P.s

*Namaste*---Hello and Goodbye, palms together of course.

*paan*---Indian snack consists of a betel leaf filled with sweet or spicy ingredients and placed inside the cheek to savor. When you first spit red, don't be alarmed…

*sadhu*---Hindu holy man. Vagrant mendicant.

*sari*—Known world-wide as an elegant feminine sheath. When my wife asked women why they wore saris, they candidly told her that they wore saris to hide their hips, so broad in the beam for most Indian women.

*Tharu*---Nepal's oldest and largest indigenous tribe whose women are known for their statuesque beauty.

Namaste, ladies.

www.ingramcontent.com/pod-product-compliance
Lightning Source LLC
Chambersburg PA
CBHW051632120626
46551CB00014B/2051